THE BERKELEY SQUARE ESTATE

EXPRESSIONS OF ELEGANCE AND EXCELLENCE

DAVID WIXON AND ALISON GRAHAM

PUBLISHED BY LANCER PROPERTY ASSET MANAGEMENT LIMITED

THE BERKELEY SQUARE ESTATE

EXPRESSIONS OF ELEGANCE AND EXCELLENCE

DAVID WIXON AND ALISON GRAHAM

PUBLISHED BY LANCER PROPERTY ASSET MANAGEMENT LIMITED

Limited Edition

Published in Great Britain, 2008
by Lancer Property Asset Management Limited
36 Berkeley Square, London W1J 6DH

ISBN 978-0-9559694-0-9

Text
David Wixon

Design and Production
Alison Graham
The London Design Factory
020 8332 2432

Photography
Chris Allerton
Christopher Allerton Photography

Additional Photography
Taylerreid Photography
The London Design Factory

Illustration
David Thompson

Picture Library Resources
Mary Evans Picture Library
The Bridgeman Art Library
The National Portrait Gallery, London
City of Westminster Archives Centre
The Worshipful Company of Painters-Stainers
Maggs Bros
Berkeley Castle Charitable Trust

Every effort has been made to trace original copyright
for all other material.

Printed by Imago in Singapore

ACKNOWLEDGEMENTS

My first acknowledgement is to Alison Graham of the London Design Factory, my equal partner in this challenging enterprise. Her great competence in all matters of design and production was matched by shrewd observations and massive encouragement when it mattered, as we gathered material. When I use the first person plural, it is Alison to whom I refer. We both in turn are grateful to Marcus Bowen, late of GVA Grimley who introduced us to Andrew Lax of Lancer. His help in defining the parameters of this project was splendid.

When presented with the remit to produce this book of such a broad canvas, it was fascinating and thoroughly unexpected to find so many coincidental meetings and commonalities as research was gradually undertaken. My own relatively recent membership of the Savile Club in Brook Street was the beginning of such experiences and meeting fellow Savilian, Robert Harding of Maggs Bros, the antiquarian book sellers of 50 Berkeley Square, ensured that I got off to a good start. We are extremely grateful to Robert and chairman Edward Maggs for their kindnesses in allowing us access not just to research material but also to No 50 Berkeley Square, the shop itself, which remains a monument to the elegance of Georgian architecture and its way of life. I also chanced to meet Maria Perry whose account of the story behind 'the nightingale' was delicately portrayed in her book *Mayfair Madams*, and I am grateful to her for allowing me to quote from her book. She represented another fascinating coincidence in that, having been commissioned to write the history of the Lansdowne Club, she received great support and encouragement from the late Colin Merton who, among other things, was librarian of the Savile Club. Mark Anderson, chief executive of the Lansdowne Club, has also been most helpful.

The next coincidence concerned the Square's eponymous hotel in Knightsbridge. Having just celebrated the sparkling life of a centenarian lady in great style at the church next door, I joined the rest of the congregation in the Berkeley Hotel to toast her memory in champagne. Here, when in conversation with Linda Jephson, she just happened to say: 'Oh, you do know that the "Nightingale" song was written for my mother and she was the first to sing it?' This represented something of a coup and we are grateful to Linda (nee Birkin) for allowing us to use the story of her mother Judy Campbell and her connection with the song.

Robert Pasley-Tyler of No 42 Berkeley Square has been more than helpful, and indeed entertaining, in briefing us on his views and experience of the area and its business. James Bowdidge, chief executive of The Property Merchant Group is not only extremely knowledgeable on matters of London's history but is also the honorary secretary of the improbable Tyburn Angling Society. On this latter subject his advice has been invaluable. I am grateful also to Antony Miller of Trehearne Architects.

John Hitchman, of architects Chapman Taylor, has been of great help as the original project architect of Lansdowne House in providing authoritative information on the most elegant of the recent additions to the Square. Albert Smith, its building manager, was most helpful as was Caroline Lammiman who arranged introductions.

We are grateful to the Westminster Archive, not just for the professional use of material but also for the facilities offered to us as members of the general public. We are also grateful to our professional 'reader' Sarah Owens.

David Wixon

A VIEW of LONDON about the Year 1560.

London c 1560. The Bridgeman Art Library.

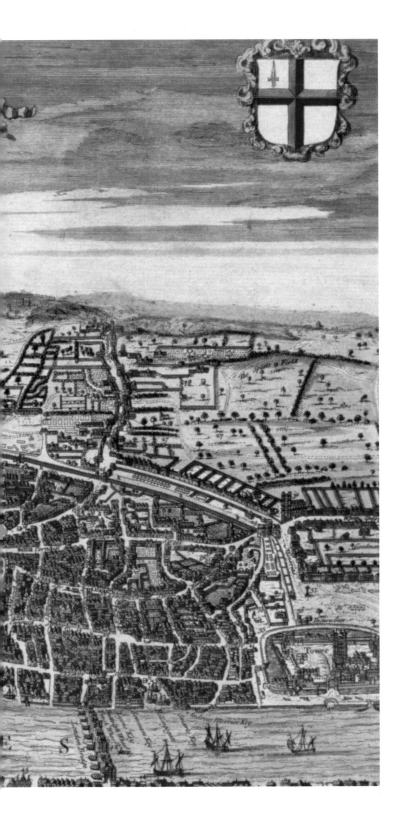

CONTENTS

Had it not been for the restoration of the monarchy under Charles II, with his light touch, his sense of humour, his love of style and quality, and the hedonism which marked his reign, it is unlikely that the West End of London would have acquired the quintessential elegance and grandeur for which it is known and has been known for over three centuries.

Charles II by Jean Baptiste Gaspars.
The Worshipful Company of Painters-Stainers.

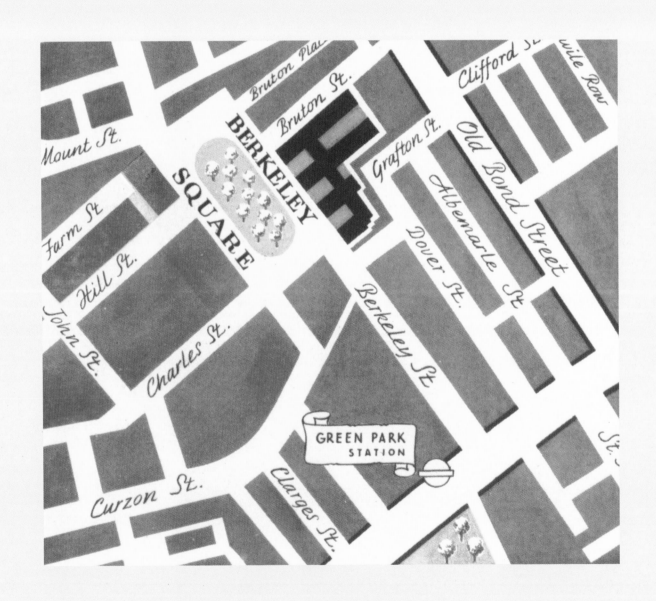

In commissioning the production of this book my partners in Lancer and I had a wish to create a publication of quality reflecting some very special real estate in an exclusive part of arguably one of the most fascinating and attractive capital cities in the world. Our brief was broad and lacking in fine definition. We know that Mayfair is one of the most sought-after addresses for both residences and businesses and we would conclude, with just a little bias, that Berkeley Square and its immediate environs epitomise that exclusivity. The brief then is to take the reader for a walk through the streets that fan out from Piccadilly with Stratton Street to the left and Berkeley Street to the right, or the east. The eastern boundary follows the unseen course of the ancient River Tyburn as it burrows its way from New Bond Street, under the Lansdowne Club and Shepherd Market, eventually to the Thames. The western boundary side-steps around the Mayfair Hotel and left towards the far end of Hill Street as it forms near enough an equilateral triangle, with Bruton Place to the right. There are those that attribute Mayfair's glittering reputation to the mistresses of great men, not least those of monarchs. Lady Castlemaine, one of Charles II's very busy mistresses did much to enhance the wild and exotic early reputation of the area, particularly as she later chose Lord Chesterfield as the centre of her attention. In all probability it was commonsense, good housekeeping and geographical advantage that were the reasons for the successful development of this approximate square mile with Regent Street one side, Park Lane the other, Oxford Street to the north and Piccadilly, the southernmost edge.

So let us take a walk in the footsteps of Lady Berkeley, the 1st Lord Berkeley's widow, and her third son, Lord William the fourth baron. We will get a feeling of the wisdom of their decision to lease their land to carpenters Cock and Hillyard who in turn built terraced housing for the rich and famous with bricks manufactured on site and made with the clay of the land first acquired by the 1st Lord Berkeley of Stratton in the mid 1600s. Great style and quality was then the order of the day. Greater style and the highest of quality is the yardstick today.

Andrew Lax

Sir Peter Lely

Iohn Berkeley

John Lord Berkeley of Stratton.

From a portrait by Sir Peter Lely at Berkeley Castle.

By permission of the Berkeley Castle Charitable Trust.

EARLY TIMES

'In sixteen hundred and sixty six
London town was burnt to sticks.'
Traditional.

The restoration of Charles II to the throne of England generated one of the most dynamic periods in the history of the United Kingdom. London's Great Plague in 1665, followed a year later by the Great Fire wreaked devastation on such a huge scale it provided almost a blank canvas for the renewal of London as a capital city. It would appear that the personality of the new King was the catalyst for the style and quality of this process. Cromwell's dour puritanical greyness was replaced by Charles's rapturous love of life. Comedy returned to the theatres, colour and extravagance dictated fashion, the Royal Society was established to promote science and philosophy and the arts flourished under wealthy patronage. This period gave rise to the birth of the great metropolis of the London that we know today. In particular Mayfair's fields and fairground were acquired by the great and the good of the time in order to establish gracious homes and estates, some of which still survive.

London is an unplanned city, growing through time as great estates closed upon each other. In the latter half of the 17th century it would appear that those loyal to the monarchy not only became rich and powerful, but also were raised with honours and title such that their families might maintain control and influence for generations to come. Three or possibly four such families were to make substantial imprints upon the land to the north and west of Piccadilly and two of them indelibly so.

With regard to the development of Mayfair in London as the centre of all that is fine and in such good taste, the role played by the first Lord Berkeley of Stratton, with his wife and family, is of prime significance. Lord Berkeley, who lived from 1607 to 1678, was born in his mother's house in Hamworth, Middlesex, the fifth son of Sir Maurice Berkeley of Bruton in Somerset. John Berkeley, already knighted in 1639 for his devoted service to Charles I, remained one of the most royal and loyal subjects during Cromwell's Commonwealth. He commanded the royalist forces successfully in Devon and Cornwall, winning a significant victory at Stratton. Samuel Pepys said of him, whilst singing his praise that, 'He fought more set fields than any man,' but later rounded upon him vigorously over his role as steward to the household of the Duke of York when he was cited for corruption. The faithful diarist records that Berkeley sold large numbers of wine licences for the Duke of York for £1,500 a year, seeing fit to pocket some £700 of that fee. Not a bad return on one's work in those days. Perhaps only Pepys saw evil in this.

Others were equal to this simple ethic of lining one's own purse. Edward Hyde, later The Earl of Clarendon, was another whose preferment was a reward for his absolute loyalty to the monarchy. He rose to become Lord Chancellor and talked the King into giving him a grant of some relatively unproductive land just north of a country road later called Piccadilly, which he was determined to sell on immediately. Had Berkeley not been able to purchase that land, providing satisfaction to both parties, then London, and particularly its West End, might never have become the jewel in London's crown that it is today.

Opposite page:
The Earl of Burlington and John, Lord Berkeley of Stratton by Sir Peter Lely. Near neighbours in 'Pickadilly'.
The Bridgeman Art Library.

This page, far right: Edward Hyde, 1st Earl of Clarendon engraved by J Cochran after Sir Peter Lely.
Mary Evans Picture Library.

This page, right: Samuel Pepys statesman and diarist.
Mary Evans Picture Library.

Said to have been a somewhat dull man, Berkeley's career is one of which any man would have been proud. Upon his gravestone in the parish church at Twickenham where he had an estate, is the legend of his quite remarkable life (see below). By any standards an outstanding man in any generation and like so many before and since, he was possessed by faults and blemishes. It was reported that he was much loved and agreeable as a young man, becoming vain and overbearing in later life.

It was not upon his marriage that his early reputation was based, for this was not to take place until he was in his early 50s. He married Christian, a twice widowed woman of substantial wealth, who was indeed much younger than him and it was hereafter that his power and influence began to exhibit itself as he and his wife positioned themselves as early day property developers. It was two hundred years before the word tycoon was introduced to the language from its original Japanese, though Berkeley would certainly have been one of the first.

Under this marble
Lye the renowned aſhes of the Right Honourable
the Ld JOHN BERKELEY, Baron of Straton, younger son
of Sir Maurice BERKELEY of Bruton in Somerſetſhire.
In the Civill wares,
In the dayes of Charles ye Iſt (for his ſignal valour and conduct
In recovering the city of Excester out of the hands of the rebels)
He was made Governer thereof & one of his Majeſty's general in ye Weſt.
Thoſe unhappy warres ended
He ſerved many campaynes in Flanders
Both in the French and Spanish armies
According as their alliances with England engaged him
After the happy Reſtauration of Charles ye 2d,
He was made Privy Counſellour, Governour of Connaught
And, after ld Lieutent of Ireland ſent twice extraordary Embaſſor
Firſt into France, 2ly to the Treaty of Nijmegen.
His other felicityes were crowned
By his happy marriage of Chriſtina, daughter of Sr: ANDREW
RICCARD
A young lady of a large Dowry and yet larger Graces and Virtues.
who alſo Enricht him with a moſt hopefull progeny.
He deceaſed
Aug ye 26, 1678, in ye 72 yeare of his Age.

Though ſprung from Danish Kings* of brightest Fame,
Whoſe Bloud and High Exploits Exalt their name,
Berkeley's own virtues moſt his Tombe doe grace,
Adde glory To, not borrow, from his Race."

*The ancient name of the Berkeleys
was Fitz-Harding, they deſcending from Eitz-Harding,
a younger ſon of the King of Denmark. E. Ironſide, 1785.

Right: Christian Lady Berkeley,
wife of John 1st Baron Berkeley of Stratton.
From a portrait by Sir Peter Lely at Berkeley Castle.

Opposite page, top: Berkeley House, Piccadilly.

Opposite page, bottom: The extent of Lord Berkeley's estate in the late 18th century, shown in pink.

Lord Berkeley built Berkeley House in the wastelands just north of the road Piccadilly. Having already purchased Brick Close, he acquired some further undeveloped land to the east called Penniless Bench from Lord Clarendon. Upon this land he built a grand house, nay a palace, Berkeley House, with its expansive gardens stretching to the north. It is this garden that forms the Berkeley Square that we have today. Shown on the plan below, the lands of Lord Berkeley are coloured pink, and the land of the Earl of Clarendon, excluding the parts that he sold immediately on becoming the owner, is hatched red. The boundaries and names in red indicate approximately the original fields.

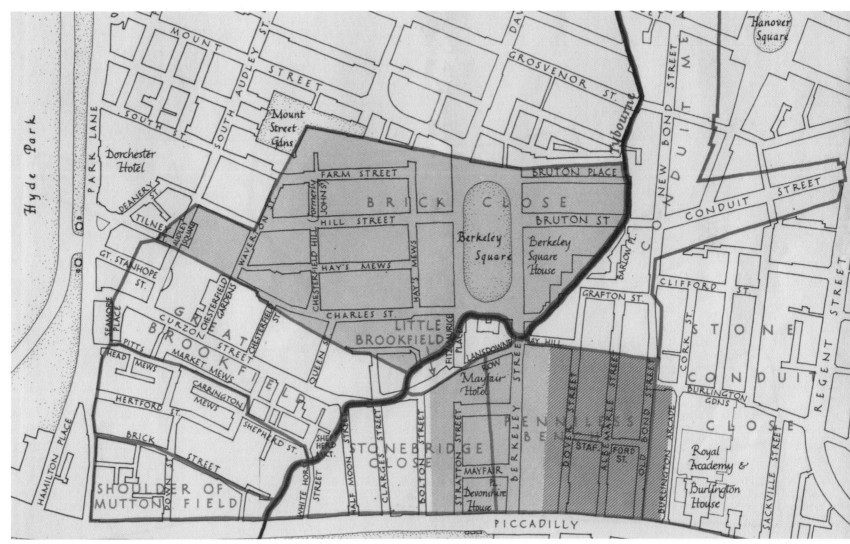

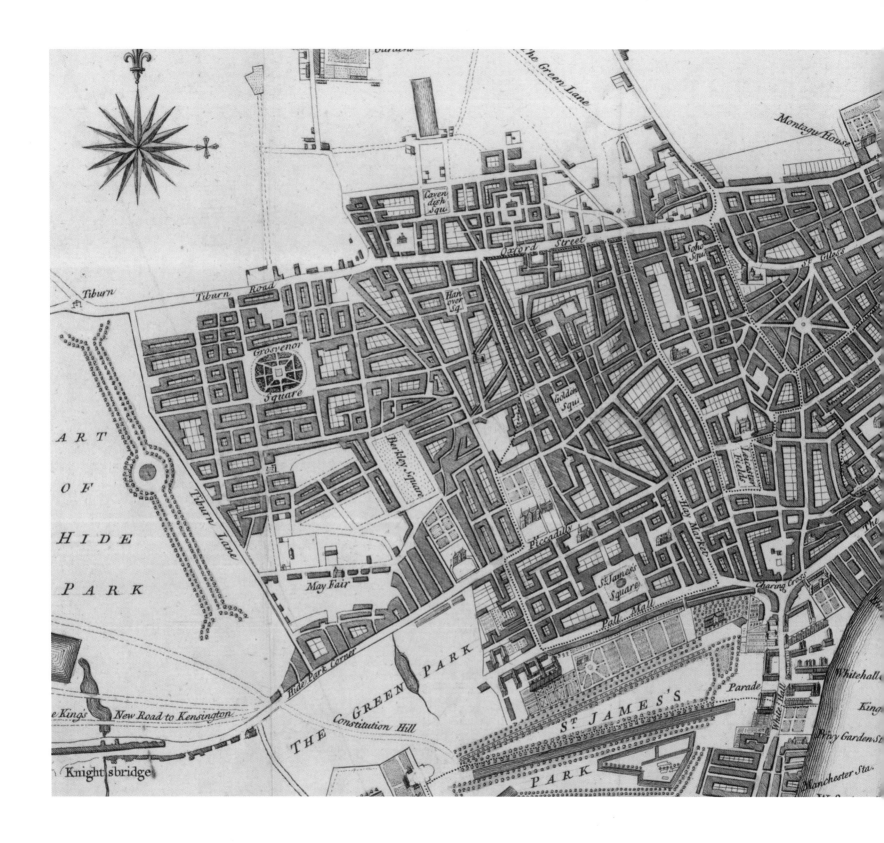

London map 1756.
Trafalgar Square does not exist, and
Mayfair is still undeveloped.
Drawn by R W Seale.
Mary Evans Picture Library.

Lord Berkeley led a life devoted to public service. Even when, by the standards of all ages, he should have led the life of a retired gentleman, he found himself first as Lord Lieutenant of Ireland and later Ambassador to France. Careful of his investment and property, he appointed a trusted agent to manage his affairs. It was during this time that he sold Berkeley House together with a relatively small garden and its freehold to the Devonshires. It is worth noting that the Berkeleys retained much of their original estate. Lord Berkeley died in 1678 and was succeeded to the Baronage by all three of his sons, two of whom pre-deceased their mother.

It was Lady Berkeley's influence and husbandry of the estate that allowed Berkeley Square to develop into the way in which we see it today. It was she who ensured that building plots were sold leasehold and, as freeholder, she was able to define the style and quality of much, if not the majority, of the housing development that took place during the second half of the 18th century and the early 19th century. Not least she was able to embrace planning regulations for the building of property, introduced after the Great Fire of London and designed to protect the properties being built for the wealthy.

As I write, and as we live our lives today, Lord Berkeley's and Lady Berkeley's monuments are a part of the daily life in London. As we shop in Bruton Street, work in Stratton Street or simply rejoice in the elegance of Berkeley Square, we do so in an area of London that pampers to the discerning whilst meeting the needs of those demanding nothing but the very best.

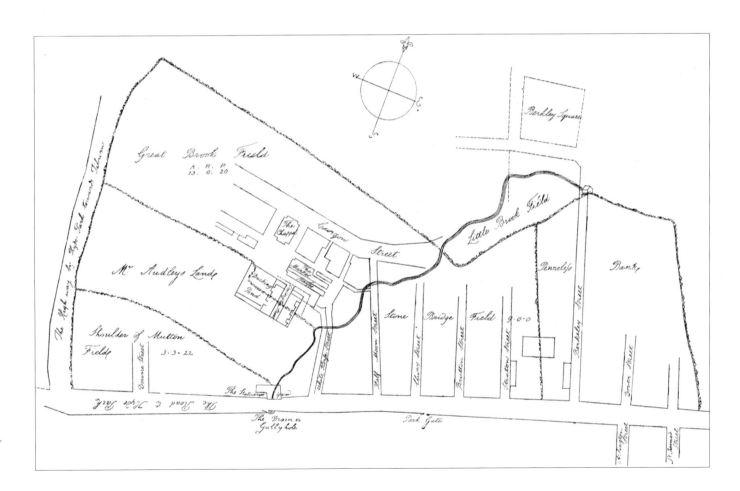

Plan of Berkeley Square Estate, about 1710.

It is likely that the reputation for style and grandeur for which this area of London became known arose not simply because of the Berkeleys but also because of three other great families or households, perhaps even four. The Burlington or Cork family, Hyde later Clarendon, and the Duke of Cambridge, with Berkeley, all chose to build four great houses along the road that ran out to the west from Piccadilly Circus to Hyde Park Corner. The western part of this road was known as Portugal Street in honour of Catherine of Braganza, wife of Charles II.

The four imposing houses were, from the east, Burlington House, Clarendon House, Berkeley House and Cambridge (later Egremont) House. Fitzmaurice, later Lansdowne, built his great house on the southwest corner of Berkeley Square, where much of it stands today as the Lansdowne Club. It is from the gardens and estates to the north of these great palaces, for that is what they were, that the most fashionable place, probably in the whole of the civilised world, began to grow.

Above left: Cambridge House in 1854.

Above right: Devonshire House in 1800.

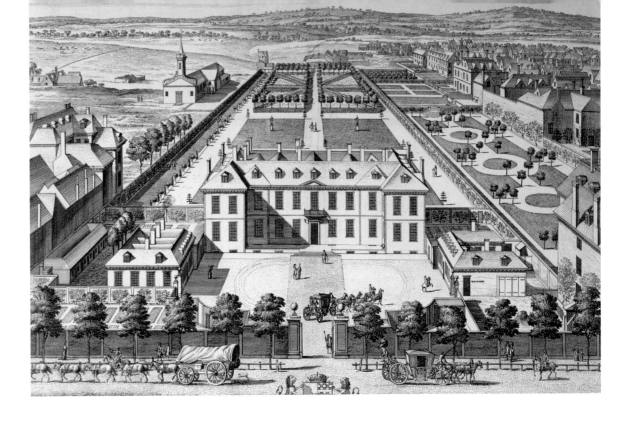

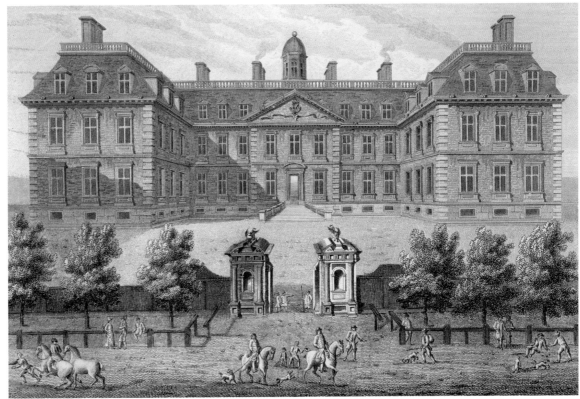

Top: Burlington House,
18th century engraving.
The Bridgeman Art Library.

Right: Clarendon House,
published 1809,
engraving by Wise.
The Bridgeman Art Library.

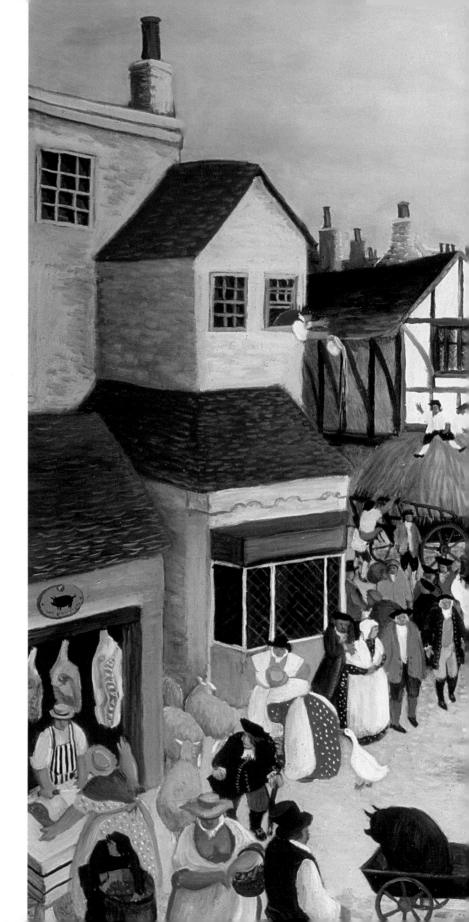

A cursory glance at street names in the *London A-Z Street Atlas* proclaims a register of the most distinguished gentlefolk of the period: Albemarle (Monck), Bond, Burlington (Cork), Curzon, Davies, Dover, Grosvenor, Jermyn and Stafford, perhaps many more such names as one looks slightly further afield from the fraction of a square mile bounded by Piccadilly, Park Lane, Oxford Street and Regent Street. For centuries this has been known as Mayfair and why not, taking as it does, its name from the two weeks of business and merry making that took place during the first two weeks of May, beginning in the reign of James II. It would have been so neat had Hyde Park been named after Edward Hyde, later Earl Clarendon, who was Lord Chancellor during Charles II reign. Whilst he did have great influence upon the development of the West End of London it is pure chance that his family name is the same as the great deer park acquired by Henry VIII from the manor of Hyde after he dissolved the monasteries.

There are streets, roads, closes, gardens and mews; all eponymous epitaphs to the investment in property and land made by the movers and shakers during the latter half of the 17th Century. The great Earl Clarendon is left with nothing, it is as though he had never been in Mayfair.

Right: Disgrace of Clarendon. Edward Hyde (Clarendon) in 1867, exiled and impeached after losing favour with Charles II over the Anglo-Dutch War.
Mary Evans Picture Library/Douglas McCarthy.

Opposite page: Nightingale engraving by an unnamed artist in 'The Animal World', 1 May 1874.
Mary Evans Picture Library.

When true lovers meet in Mayfair,
So the legends tell,
Song-birds sing; winter turns to spring.
Every winding street in Mayfair falls beneath the spell.
I know such enchantment can be,
'Cause it happened one evening to me.

That certain night, the night we met,
There was magic abroad in the air,
There were angels dining at the Ritz,
And a nightingale sang in Berkeley Square.

27

In 1940 with Great Britain still in the first year of the Second World War an extraordinarily beautiful woman, in a revue called *New Faces* at the Comedy Theatre was to make her mark in the history of light entertainment, if not the history of a nation. Judy Campbell was an unknown actress from the Liverpool Rep recruited into a revue by the relatively well-known theatre impresario Eric Maschwitz. She was to have rendered a monologue by Dorothy Parker that was somehow mislaid and it was that simple mischance that gave birth to this legend.

Maschwitz, a member of the Savile Club, was a songwriter as well as an impresario in show business. He got to know a certain Armenian émigré, improbably called Dikran Kouyoumdjian, who came to London after the First World War and it is this man who is surely responsible for the Berkeley Square nightingale enigma. Kouyoumdjian was obsessed by the British upper middle classes who sported themselves extravagantly in the clubs of Mayfair as they shook off the horrors of this terrible war. He changed his name to Michael Arlen and wrote stories about the demi-monde of Mayfair, its streets, its shops, its bars and its clubs. In all probability it was by accident that he created the myth when in a book of his called *These Charming People* written in 1923, he included a story 'When the Nightingale Sang in Berkeley Square'. Reports suggest that Eric Maschwitz had worked with Arlen dramatising one or some of his stories for the stage, when he came across 'the nightingale'. Apparently it was not such a great story.

Maria Perry, in her book *Mayfair Madams*, has little time for the triangle of passion arising from Michael Arlen's original story of the heroine, the cuckold and the lover, all caricatures of what must then have been the equivalent of the 'chattering classes'. She gives the butler in the piece a nod of approval though his fame is but short lived!

Eric Maschwitz was not at all fazed at having lost the Dorothy Parker monologue. He had up his sleeve a neat little song with a longish title, 'A nightingale sang in Berkeley Square'. Having had thoughts of asking Vera Lynn to use it, he simply suggested to Judy Campbell that she should include it in her act. By her own admission, Miss Campbell could not sing and she did not sing the song, she performed it.

It was an instant success. Her obituary in *The Daily Telegraph* in 2002 said: 'Anxious lest her small, husky voice should not carry in a theatre without microphones, she half talked, half laughed, half whispered, wholly croaked her way through the song; then threw her boa in the air and walked off. Her performance brought the house down and the show ran for more than a year.'

Recordings were costly and even rationed throughout those days during the war. The first contemporary recordings were by Vera Lynn and Bing Crosby. Those who care and understand know that it was Judy Campbell's song and she was without any doubt one of the most beautiful, elegant and enchantingly feminine players of her generation; such a sentiment no doubt would have been endorsed by Noel Coward with whom she appeared in many plays.

I may be right, I may be wrong,
But I'm perfectly willing to swear
That when you turned and smiled at me,
A nightingale sang in Berkeley Square.

Michael Arlen

Above: Michael Arlen.
Mary Evans Picture Library.

Right: Judy Campbell.
Mander & Mitchenson Theatre Collection.

The moon that lingered over London town,
Poor puzzled moon, he wore a frown.
How could he know we two were so in love?
The whole darn world seemed upside down.
The streets of town were paved with stars;
It was such a romantic affair.
And, as we kissed and said goodnight,
A nightingale sang in Berkeley Square.

How strange it was, how sweet and strange;
There was never a dream to compare
With that hazy, crazy night we met
When a nightingale sang in Berkeley Square.

Above: The original sheet music for 'A Nightingale sang in Berkeley Square'.

Right: World War II songs published at the time by 'Picture Post'.

There is a scratchy copy of a wax recording of this song by Judy Campbell in her early twenties. It is haunting, wistful, delicate and yet powerful. It prompted Harold Hobson to write at a time when bombs rained nightly down upon London: 'Judy Campbell … lifted the fear out of my heart and out of the hearts of five hundred people … and what amazing pressure of collected happiness she would put into her agreeable, husky voice as she sang the words now so familiar.'

The *Reader's Digest Book of British Birds* has it: 'For every ten people who have ever heard a nightingale sing there can hardly be one who has actually set eyes on this shy bird.'

Miss Perry writes: 'The BBC played it and Glenn Miller made a best-selling record. Vera Lynn, the Forces' Sweetheart, sang it and the girls dishing out steaming cups of NAAFI tea to the young men going to the Front who hummed it, as did the nurses bandaging the young men who came back.'

'London during the Blitz', she goes on to say: 'the nightclubs were full of soldiers on leave and wives and sweethearts flocked to the capital to meet them. The haunting refrain of the nightingale song seemed like a message of hope, even though Maschwitz's lyrics proclaimed it unlikely any bird would sing in a Berkeley Square blacked out against air raids with its railings melted down in armaments factories. The dancers didn't heed the words, they just sang the tune.'

When dawn came stealing up all gold and blue,
To interrupt our rendezvous,
I still remember how you smiled and said,
'Was that a dream or was it true?'
Our homeward step was just as light
As the tap-dancing feet of Astaire
And, like an echo far away,
A nightingale sang in Berkeley Square.

A nightingale may never have sung in Berkeley Square before and may never sing there again but, if it does, it will probably mean something.

The last word is Judy Campbell's:

I know, 'cause I was there,
That night in Berkeley Square.

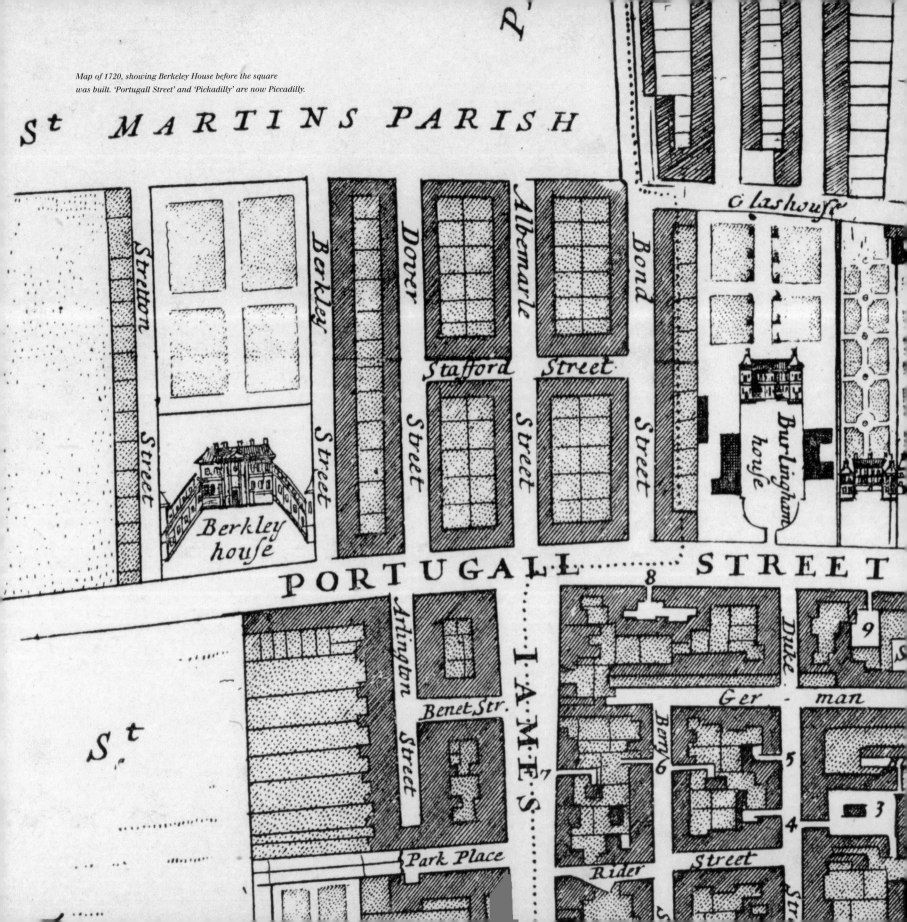

Map of 1720, showing Berkeley House before the square was built. 'Portugall Street' and 'Pickadilly' are now Piccadilly.

St M A R T I N S P A R I S H

Stretton Street

Berkley Street

Berkley house

Dover Street

Stafford Street

Albemarle Street

Bond Street

Glashouse

Burlingham house

P O R T U G A L L . . . . S T R E E T

8

Arlington Street

Benet Str.

Park Place

I · A · M · E · S

7

Duke Str.

German street

Berry

9

5

6

4

Rider street

S.t

3

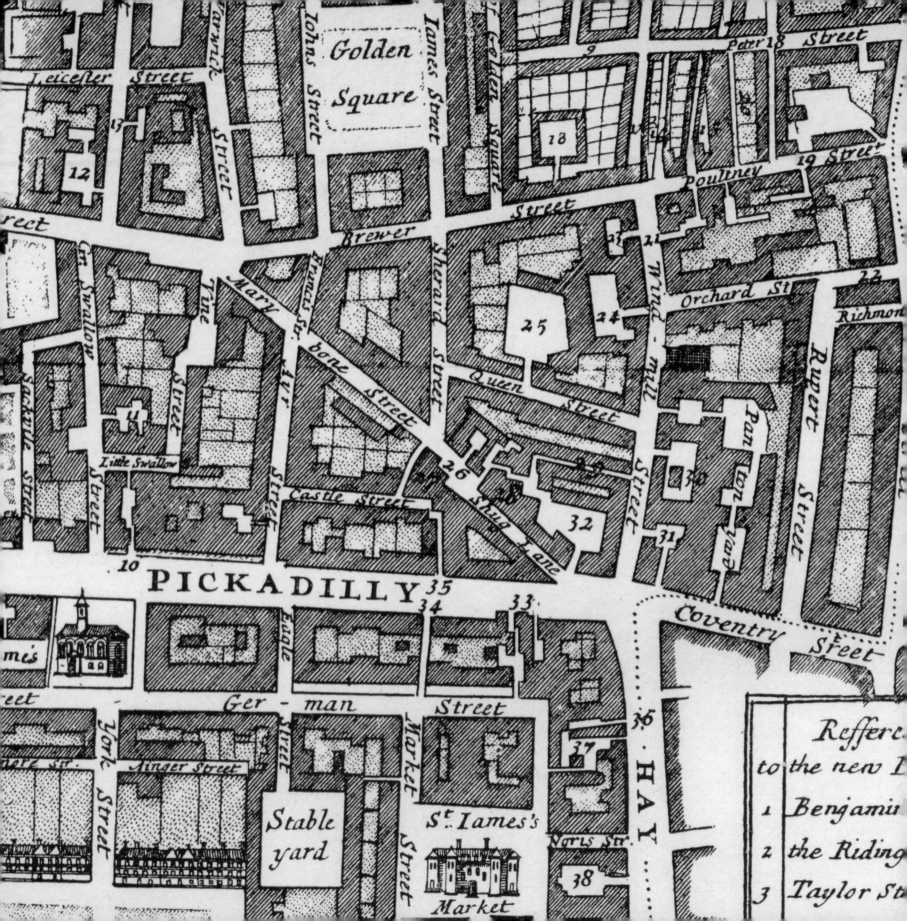

Right: Berkeley Square, Devonshire House and Lansdowne House and their gardens in 1916.

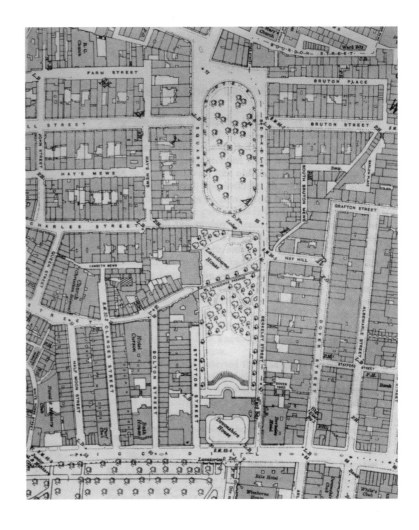

*'Let me take you by the hand
and lead you through the streets of London.'*
Lyrics, Ralph McTell.

With 'cash for honours' invading the headlines of every newspaper at the beginning of the 21st century, it is not easy to see how the super rich in contemporary life can immortalise their place or role in the history of the world. In the 17th and 18th centuries it was achievable and it was done. High honours and great wealth, however they were acquired, separately or jointly, were sufficient for any man or indeed woman to leave his or her mark upon earth for close to eternity. The streets of London, and particularly Mayfair, give testimony to this. These chances for marking the card of history appeared to be available to only a relatively small group of Londoners who lived between about 1650 to 1750.

ALBEMARLE STREET

Albemarle Street takes its name from the 2nd Duke of Albemarle son of George Monck one of the earliest great warriors of the 17th century. Monck was raised to the dukedom after the restoration of the monarchy. He was a military general upon land and sea and probably the very first fighting admiral, although the name and rank had yet to be brought into common usage. It was his son, the 2nd Duke, who bought Clarendon House, pulling it down and leasing it to a John Hinde, who with Thomas Bond, Henry Jermyn, Margaret Stafford and others, developed the area further.

AUDLEY STREETS NORTH AND SOUTH

Hugh Audley (or even Awdeley, as his name was sometimes spelt) weaves a convoluted path through the great families who were responsible mainly for building the part of London known latterly as West One or simply W1. Audley was senior clerk in the City, who doubled as a moneylender, and in his day acquired immense wealth. He was uncle to the Davies family who were fleetingly involved with the Berkeleys, intimately integrated with the Grosvenors, and associated with the manor of Eye or Eia that became the Ebury Estate.

BARLOW PLACE

This street is named after master carpenter Thomas Barlow, builder of a number of properties in the area including Bourdon House in Davies Street.

Above: George Monck, Duke of Albermarle
'Captain General of all his Majesties Land forces'.
Engraved by Bartolozzi, 1796.
Mary Evans Picture Library.

Opposite page, right: South Audley Street.

BERKELEY SQUARE

Whilst taking its name from the Berkeley Estate of her husband the 1st Lord Berkeley, it was Lady Berkeley and her third son, William, the 4th Lord Berkeley (some say it was John the 5th Lord Berkeley, Lady Berkeley's grandson), who leased their land to carpenters Messrs Cock and Hillyard for the development of housing. Within that lease was the provision that the original gardens to the north of their Berkeley House should remain free of buildings. The wish was honoured and houses were built on both sides and the garden. The Berkeleys' garden is the Berkeley Square we see today.

BERKELEY STREET AND STRATTON STREET

John the 1st Lord Berkeley of Stratton built his splendid palace, Berkeley House, on the road out of London to Exeter, called for a brief period of time Portugal Street and later Piccadilly (Pickadilly even). He built streets either side of his garden: to the east Berkeley Street and to the west Stratton Street, named after his distinguished victory at Stratton in Cornwall during the Civil War.

Left: Sir William Berkeley, Vice Admiral.
National Portrait Gallery, London.

Above: John Berkeley, 1st Baron of Stratton.
National Portrait Gallery, London.

Opposite page: Berkeley Square.

BOLTON STREET

Bolton Street takes its name from the Duke of Bolton who most famously in 1696 had sewer pipes laid to serve his properties. In 1708 this street was the most western in London.

BOURDON STREET

Little is known of William Bourdon who built his house on Davies Street. Bourdon Street provided access to his land.

Right: Charles Paulet,
1st Duke of Bolton. Statesman.
National Portrait Gallery, London.

Opposite page: Bond Street.

BOND STREET

Sir Thomas Bond was a speculator buying much if not all Albemarle Grounds from the eponymous 2nd Duke in 1683. He leaves a remarkable legacy in that he survived only two more years, during which time he leased this land for further development (see Albemarle Street). He created Bond Street which later became Old Bond Street and it was not until 1736 that it was extended by the building of New Bond Street, becoming the only street stretching the breadth of Mayfair from north to the south. It is of note that Admiral Lord Nelson once lived in Bond Street.

BRUTON STREET AND BRUTON PLACE

It is of some great significance that Lord John Berkeley of Stratton's family, which came to its demise with the death of the 5th Baron in 1773, should leave their family mark upon four of the streets connecting with Berkeley Square. The 1st Baron Berkeley was born the fifth son of Sir Maurice Berkeley of Bruton, Somerset. This particular branch of the family lasted for only two generations. The 2nd, 3rd and 4th Barons were all sons of the 1st Lord Berkeley and the 5th, his grandson, was a bachelor.

BURLINGTON ARCADE AND GARDENS, OLD BURLINGTON STREET, CLIFFORD AND CORK STREET

The 1st Earl of Burlington bought the house that subsequently took his name on the northern side of Piccadilly. The Burlingtons, the Cliffords and the Boyles, who were also Corks and Orrerys, were all interlinked by marriage and various elevations of rank such that, over a short period of time, during the early part of the 18th century, their names were translated into the posterity of the geography of London.

CHARLES STREET

It is tempting to consider this street being named in honour of Charles II whose style and philosophy inspired the development of this area of London. However, Charles was Lady Berkeley's second son, the 3rd Lord Berkeley. It is thought he is the source of this name for the street. Incidentally, there is a Charles II Street in SW1.

CLARGES STREET

It is likely that Sir Thomas Clarge, who died in 1691, gives his name to this street, though it was not built upon until the early 1700s. Most famous among its inhabitants must surely be Lady Hamilton. Perhaps it was more than just chance that brought the great Lord Nelson to live close by in Bond Street. Interestingly, Clarges Street is one of the few streets to use the possessive form of the sponsor's name. Even then, it is grammatically inaccurate in failing to include the apostrophe, to become Clarge's Street.

CHESTERFIELD STREET, HILL AND GARDENS

In all probability it was the 4th Earl of Chesterfield for whom these parts of London were named, not least because of his fondness for the mistress of King Charles II, one Lady Castlemaine who lived in Chesterfield Hill. This road runs north from Charles Street and was, until 1940, called John Street, John being a name much used by the original Berkeley family, there being three such Lords Berkeley.

Opposite page, top right: Burlington Arcade published 1819.

Opposite page, bottom right: Richard Boyle, 1st Earl of Burlington and
2nd Earl of Cork (1612-1698).
He was Lord High Treasurer of Ireland.
National Portrait Gallery, London.

Opposite page, bottom left: His wife, Catherine Fenton Countess of Cork c 1590.
Mary Evans Picture Library.

Above: Philip Dormer Stanhope, 4th Earl of Chesterfield
(1694-1773). Statesman.
National Portrait Gallery, London.

Above: One Curzon Street.

DAVIES STREET

Davies Street was named after Mary Davies, the heiress who, by her marriage at the age of twelve and a half years to Sir Thomas Grosvenor in 1677, took her London estate into the Grosvenor family. It is of note that there was a possibility of this distinguished lady marrying into the Berkeley family after an attempt at a pre-pubescent betrothal to the young Charles Berkeley. Davies Street was developed principally as the return frontages of large building plots that faced onto the main east-west streets. These plots were made available to builders by several agreements between 1720 and 1723. Initially it was envisaged that good-class houses would be built along the street and most of the early agreements contained a long list of restricted uses, but by 1723 these had been reduced to only the most obnoxious trades such as brewing or tallow melting, although stables and coach-houses were built on part of its frontage.

CURZON STREET (FORMERLY BLICK STREET)

Curzon Street travels the length of what was Great Brookfield, taking its name from Sir Nathanial Curzon who in the early 1700s was in considerable dispute with the Berkeley family over the ownership of two acres of land called Little Brickfield. The Curzons won the case and leased the land towards the rear of Lansdowne House to a joiner called Blick and it was for him, an artisan, that the street was first named. Nathanial was an ancestor of the very famous Marquis Curzon, Viceroy of India and nearly Prime Minister in 1923.

Henry Lord Jermyn.
The original Picture is at Strawberry Hill.

His Autograph from an original Letter in the Possession of
John Thane.

Right: Henry Lord Jermyn, Earl of St Albans, courtier, in exile during the commonwealth (1604-1684).
Mary Evans Picture Library.

DOVER STREET AND JERMYN STREET

Henry Jermyn, nephew of Henry Jermyn Earl of St Albans, had associations with both the Bond and Berkeley families through the marriage of kinsfolk. He was prominent at the court of Charles II, though not always favourably, particularly so when diverting the favours of the King's mistress, the Lady Castlemaine. Later created Lord Dover, he left two streets named: one for his family name and one for his title.

LANSDOWNE ROW AND FITZMAURICE PLACE

It is not easy to understand quite why the Shelburne family, whose 2nd Earl later became the 1st Marquess of Lansdowne in 1766, are not commemorated with more distinguished thoroughfares in and around Berkeley Square. It may of course be that the exotic Lansdowne House was simply stranded and sandwiched within the greater estate of the Berkeleys. Fitzmaurice was their family name providing them with a modest touch of immortality, but not until 1930 when the house, and its gardens, was sold for development.

Above: William Petty, 1st Marquess of Lansdowne (Lord Shelburne).
Prime Minister and patron of the arts.
National Portrait Gallery, London.

Above: Lansdowne Row.
Separating Lansdowne House from the Mayfair Hotel.

SHEPHERD STREET AND MARKET

Shepherd Market is most famously cited as the site of the original May Fair. It is named after Edward Shepherd, an architect and builder, who developed the site from about 1735. The more distinguished residents were very pleased by this development as it eventually put paid to the riotous and rowdy behaviour of the revellers who sported themselves annually at the fair. Shepherd Market should never be referred to as Shepherd's Market.

STAFFORD STREET

Margaret Stafford was an unmarried lady of considerable wealth and influence from a distinguished Northamptonshire family. In the late 17th century she was to partner Sir Thomas Bond in the development of what was Clarendon House. On an inside wall of the Duke of Albemarle public house, on the corner of Stafford Street with Albemarle Street, is the historic street sign dated 1686.

Above: The Stafford Street sign, 1686: preserved in 'The Duke of Albemarle', Stafford Street.

Right: Remains of Clarendon House, Three Kings Livery Stables, 1851.

The Bridgeman Art Library.

THE SQUARE

'There is very little squareness about Berkeley Square.'
Max Beerbohm 1912.

The plane trees in the square were planted in 1789 by Edward Bouverie, a resident of No 13. House numbering immediately arises as a problem, because at some point in time they were clearly changed, there being clear alternative evidence that Mr Bouverie lived at No 24 (the same house). To add to a little confusion, there are references stating that houses were not numbered at all but simply identified by a brass plaque inscribed with the owner's name. Bouverie's planting of the plane trees was indeed enlightened, as the flaking bark of the tree absorbs pollutants in the atmosphere, preventing damage to the trees. This could hardly have been known at the time. So novel were the plane trees with their mottled bark, that Charles II was concerned that the trees were diseased and might die. Their elegance is much enhanced because there is little else to distract those who relax on the benches, many of which were donated by Americans. There are just two statues, an elegant classical water nymph by Alexander Munro, which was commissioned by the 3rd Marquess of Lansdowne, and a plinth, upon which sculptures are placed from time to time. A while ago a charming but unlikely representation of the female form, seemingly of striated stone discs, was there. Before that a bronze horse's head and afterwards, a shiny, bronze, bulbous Isis of a bird, with a long beak and no explanation.

A decidous tree, the London plane tree is grown in town and city streets, parks and gardens in most of central and western Europe. The wood is fine grained and makes a good veneer.

The square was the site of what must be considered one of the greatest failures in the world of sculpture and statuary. Commissioned by Princess Amelia, the statue was that of her father, King George III, mounted and depicted as the Roman General, Marcus Aurelius and thought to be the work of French sculptor Beaupré, as directed by the King's sculptor Joseph Wilton. By an error of judgement and lack of metallurgical competence, the vast statue was cast in lead with legs unable to support the massive weight of the King and his mount. Over the years, the legs eventually buckled and the statue was removed in 1827. In its place is the quaint little pump house we see today, a slightly odd building surmounted by an ornamental cup.

Spring in the square brings a golden rush of daffodills, mixed with a haze of bluebells and crocus. Gardeners tend to the lawns and plane tree leaves emerge as a pale green canopy. The park benches become occupied at lunchtime and make good pickings for small birds, as crumbs fall from the sandwiches of the office workers.

The Summer Ball in Berkeley Square might still hold claim to being one of the most sought-after invitation cards to nestle over the fireplaces of the socially active. Over the years the style and purpose has changed. It derives from the great debutante ball, originally honouring the birthday of Queen Charlotte, wife of George III. Known affectionately as 'Lottie's Hop', it survived for nearly 200 years, when the 18-year-old daughters of the well-to-do were presented at court and 'came out' into society.

Nowadays the balls are centered upon raising money for charity, with the Prince's Trust and Land Aid among recent beneficiaries. The lawns are covered by colourful marquees, great chefs with more stars than an American army general create multi-course gourmet menus for the several hundred guests and new specialists on the block, mixologists, devise and invent original and powerful cocktails for them as they arrive.

Administration and maintenance of the square
is under the control of Westminster Council,
who leases it from the owners. Winter is thus a
good time to tidy up the square for the spring
ahead, by clearing leaves, tending to edges,
raking the gravel and repairing benches.

God bless the master of this house,
God bless the mistress too,
And all around the table.

God rest ye merry, gentlemen ... and ladies and
hedge fund managers and couturiers and
gallery curators and office workers and club
goers and publicans and discerning car owners
and postmen and those that eat sandwiches on
the benches.

At Christmas time each year the square is
brightened by a large festive tree. Activities in
the square increase pre-Christmas, as special
events, dinners and charity evenings are held
under marquees on the lawns.

CLUBS AND CLUBLAND

'With spots quadrangular of di'mond form,
Ensanguin'd hearts, clubs typical of strife,
And spades, the emblem of untimely graves.'
The Task, The Winter Evening, William Makepeace Thackeray.

There is a desire to identify the world of clubs and clubland as an entity, bestowing upon Berkeley Square and Mayfair as a whole, a special air or significance. An essential feature of a club is that it is exclusive; the word club is synonymous with exclusion. The presence, therefore, of a relatively small number of clubs, means only that it is the clubs themselves that benefit from the reputation established by the area over the centuries. The common denominator is the relatively high threshold of personal wealth and celebrity required on the part of those using such facilities.

The word club in the context of entertainment, food, drink and sometimes accommodation, possesses a wide spectrum of meaning. The word is hewn from the rock of legal definition over the centuries, to overcome various laws aimed at protecting individuals from themselves. It is not surprising therefore, that many such clubs were formed with the aim of increasing the availability and use of alcohol or to allow gambling. It is but a small step thereafter to define the question of with whom one should enjoy such privileges.

At the present time, even though there are hardly any prohibitions or restrictions in any area of normal activity that include drinking, gaming and betting, the concept of the club survives, even thrives. In its purest form, clearly a matter for conjecture, there is the so-called gentleman's club. Just touching the loose boundaries of this area is the Savile Club in Brook Street, described as one of the most prestigious private clubs in Britain, having been established in 1868 and occupying a fine 18th century house. Its distinguished history has made it famous within Britain's literary, academic and artistic circles and remains a vibrant, flourishing traditional men's club to this day.

Proudly displaying its Union Flag is the Naval Club at 38 Hill Street, originally the RNVR Club. The building is dedicated as a War Memorial to those members of the Naval Volunteer Reserve Forces from the then British Empire, who gave their lives on active service during the Second World War. It opens its doors to all who have an interest in, or love of, the sea.

Contributing to the theme of the Armed Forces, the Naval & Military Club, originally housed in what was Cambridge, and later Egremont House at the western end of Piccadilly, survived until just a few years ago. It was known affectionately as the 'In & Out' because of the obvious way in which the two gates were marked. This feature is so engrained in the tradition of the club, that after its removal to St James' Square, the single doorway boldly boasts 'In' on the right hand porch column and 'Out' on the left one.

The Lansdowne Club can be found in Fitzmaurice Place, the building is imposing and fulfilling of all the promise derived from its fascinating history. Its style has always been on the front foot of social activity. It was a mixed (male and female) club from its beginnings on the other side of the square when it was the Bruton Club. (It seems odd to write such a statement in the 21st century.) The decor is spectacularly art deco and redolent of the Atlantic Ocean liners of the 1920s and, with that, a lingering hint of naughtiness hanging in the air. Perhaps this latter is down to Mr Selfridges' tenants, the Dolly Sisters, two famous flappers of the 1920s whose reputations may have contributed to this feeling. The Lansdowne Club did much to enhance standards in the sporting world post-war and particularly so with swimming and squash.

In between the archetypal London club and the broader base of ones such as the Lansdowne, there is the private business club. Robert Pasley Tyler identifies his club at 42 Berkeley Square as being unique and indeed it most probably is. Its membership identifies the manner in which it is run, and that is for the personal benefit of individual members. They are free to relax or pursue their business aims as they see fit in the most elegant style of an 18th century town house.

At the top of the Square is Morton's. Who is or was Mr Morton? It is not an easy question to have answered. Their website will proclaim, with little modesty: 'Quality venue. Quality service. Quality food. Quality crowd.'

Where does the English Speaking Union (ESU) fit within this massive spectrum of selectivity? Dartmouth House in Charles Street is home to the ESU within an important heritage building. It was sumptuously remodelled and refurbished in the 1890s by Lord Revelstoke, who created a grand town mansion in the Anglo-French style. The building, noted for its magnificent interior with grand marble fireplaces, Louis Quatorze walnut panelling, the fine French marble grand staircase with its superb painted ceiling by Pierre Victor Galland, all seem at odds with its simple calling. The ESU was formed to promote international understanding and cooperation through the use of the English language. It boasts the highest quality cuisine and, I suspect, possibly the lowest membership fees for facilities of such quality.

The northern end of the square at night.
Vibrant and busy with Morton's as a popular
night-time haunt.

Gambling goes on apace in and around Berkeley Square. One only needs a modest grade pass in GCSE Maths to conclude that the odds in any event upon which folk gamble are stacked in favour of the bank. It is therefore, not surprising, to note that the finest property in Berkeley Square is the Clermont Club where folk not only gamble, but do so for very high stakes. The Blue Moon in Berkeley Street, allied to Crockfords in Curzon Street, has a reputation for style and quality for those who are fond of gambling. Whilst membership is a requirement of these clubs, it can be achieved in 24 hours, unlike the London Clubs where proposal and seconding of candidates is essential and black balling signifies a lack of success.

Finally, at the end of any day, there are the nightclubs, offering style, music, food, wine, sometimes cabaret and romance (bring your own romance). Famously there is Annabel's situated below the Clermont Club with a reputation pre-eminent among all nightclubs in London and possibly the world. Even now after many years, those who know, will think of the original Annabel and recall her fine figure marvelling at the longevity of such a reputation. There is also Babble in Lansdowne House boasting individual curtained booths ensuring privacy, they say, from the dance floor. They do not say why this is such a marketable facility. Does one see a dwarfish little man in a bowler hat going from booth to booth myopically peering over his sketchpad through pebble pince-nez? I think not. Then round the corner into Berkeley Street is the Funky Buddha (FB); well how funky can you get. The FB advertising suggests that it is the fat besuited men who make their way to Annabel's whilst the bon chic bon gens in the guise of sexy socialites, slink past the doormen of the FB and downstairs to the delights therein. Some fine clubs have departed from the area and, by chance, three from Charles Street. The Guards Club, almost enshrined at No 16, which still has the carved initials GS above the door, have amalgamated with the Cavalry Club nearer Piccadilly. The Cosmopolitan Club was at No 30, founded in 1851 by Sir Robert Morcom for 'good conversation and exchange of ideas', is now long forgotten.

Guests arriving at Annabel's by taxi whilst traffic zips past Jack Barclay's, and Lansdowne House where Babble also draws nightime clubbers and socialites.

In Georgian times monarchs would choose to invite themselves to the homes of favoured residents, particularly those on the west side of the square. The gateways of four of these houses incorporate inverted horns high up to the right and left. These were fitted so that running footmen, otherwise linkmen, were able to dowse their flaming torches or links.

52 BERKELEY SQUARE

The owners and residents may easily be traced from 1745 to the present day with names that gently shake the tree of history such as Cavendish, even a Boothby, and in 1874 Hugh Rose, Field Marshal Lord Strathnairn, lived there. He was one of the generals chiefly responsible for suppressing the Indian Mutiny and died in 1885 at the age of 84. It was originally built by Cock and Hillyard as a small two-storey house and leased at first to a Lady Day in 1740, initially for a peppercorn rent.

In 1838, surgeon Thomas Nicholson took over occupancy, trying without initial success to increase the size of the house. Planning permission seemed as difficult to obtain in the 19th century as it was in the late 20th. By 1885 the house had fallen into a state of ill repair when it was put up for sale. The architect Sir Mervyn Macartney bought No 52 and lived there for four years during which time he developed No 52A as a separate three-storey property, eventually making it his home and office until 1905. The last resident of No 52 was a Mrs Montrose Cloete and in 1949 the property became offices for a company working within the petroleum industry.

Above: Gateway in 1840.
City of Westminster Archives Centre.

Left: Detail of the wrought iron link extinguisher.

Opposite page: (From right to left) 50, 51 and 52 Berkeley Square.

51 BERKELEY SQUARE

It is fascinating and almost bizarre how little there is to say about No 51. A 1993 surveyor's report contains four pages on the history of Berkeley Square and but one paragraph on that of the house. Even then, it simply states that, having belonged to the Duchess of Bedford, it was converted from residential use to a bank in 1936.

52A BERKELEY SQUARE

Hans Stanley succeeded Sir Mervyn Macartney to live at No 52A. He was at one time a Civil Lord of the Admiralty and also Governor of the Isle of Wight.

Internationally renowned and pre-eminent, antiquarian bookseller Maggs Bros is housed in No 50 Berkeley Square where they have been for about half of their existence. In 1870, Uriah Maggs defined the main thrust of his business as, 'Second-hand books, Ancient and Modern, in all classes of literature'. The house is as close to the original build as it can be and the rooms are fitted with bookshelves taken from Maggs' earlier shops first in Paddington Green and later Conduit Street. The Adam fireplaces are there, the kitchen range is there, and even the tunnel connecting the mews quarters of the staff is original though now used for storage. Even today, the office space for Maggs' military specialist is confined within the original iron-railed partitions of the Georgian loose boxes in the stable block. The mews building has a rare false, or modesty wall, designed to prevent the servants from overlooking the activities of the family.

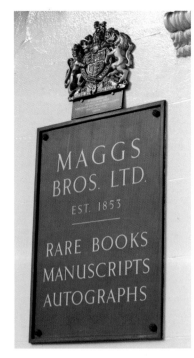

The house has a fascinating history. The first owners were said not to have occupied No 50, visiting only twice yearly and locking their servants in the basement for the period of the visit. There are many tales from the 19th century of folk succumbing to ghostly manifestations of several kinds. The present tenants use and occupy every room in the house quite comfortably and without fear. Certainly, the most distiguished and probably the sanest of all the previous inhabitants was George Canning. Canning entered Parliament in 1793 as a disciple of William Pitt. He is remembered as the architect of Britain's liberal foreign policy after the Napoleonic Wars. Canning clashed with Lord Castlereagh over war strategy and fought a duel with him in 1809. He was Foreign Secretary a number of times before he was appointed PrimeMinister in 1827.

Just to enter Maggs Bros is an experience. For some reason it has an aura, combining the smell of history with the spirit of learning. Consultant specialists beaver away upon desks strewn with papers, books and other references in every room on every floor with only the presence of a PC to acknowledge the 21st century. Were it not its prime business the Maggs Bros inventory of antiquarian books would best be described as priceless. Perhaps their most historic achievement was to acquire from a penniless Russian government of the 1930s not only a Gutenberg Bible of 1455 but also the Codex Sinaiticus, of AD 350, the earliest known of all Bible manuscripts.

Even today, you may be seen by Ed Maggs, great, great grandson of the founder, Uriah. He specialises in modern books and is managing director.

45 BERKELEY SQUARE

Below left: No 48 in 1887, then the London home of the Marquesses of Bath.

Below right: No 48 today.

Lord Clive, known throughout history as Clive of India, bought this house in 1774. It was said of him that he was a man: 'who in twenty years of his life, he saved a province, conquered a kingdom and oversaw order for anarchy and introduced justice for violence'. This was the last private house that still had its owner's name engraved on a brass plate on the door, as was the custom before numbering began. It was inscribed 'Earl of Powis', Clive's son, and is now on the study door in Powis Castle. Clive died in distressing circumstances from an overdose of laudanum. Today, the house is forlorn, empty and unloved. Interestingly it was at one time used as the headquarters of supporters of the Moral Rearmament movement.

No 44 seems to be a great focus for Berkeley Square. Many an artist determined to capture the spirit of the square will sit on a bench in the square opposite the Clermont Club, with Annabel's below, and capture its frontage. The fine Georgian house seems scarred by the daunting sentry box at the top of the cellar steps, giving a lie to the potential pleasure and laughter that might await those descending. Meanwhile, Lady Isabella Finch's great house stands proudly aloof and aloft. Shortly after it was built, it was described as one of the most elegant of terraced houses and Hugh Walpole as an early visitor described its staircase as 'the most beautiful piece of scenery', presumably in the world.

This was the home of Lady Blandford, a busy socialite of the mid 1700s. A frequent dinner guest, but clearly doubtful friend, wrote of an evening with Lady Blandford in this hardly complementary way: 'I never saw her have a worse dinner; a great round of boiled beef, little mutton pyes, beans and bacon, and mackerel without fennel sauce. The second course, a neck of lamb, a gooseberry pye, and two other little things, not meat. You know I am not difficult, and yet I was at a loss to make my dinner. Boiled beef is a good thing, but a dish I seldom eat and little mutton pyes are too savoury: beans I hate and mackerel without fennel sauce, I cannot eat.' My! What a friend!

42 BERKELEY SQUARE

No 42 was built for the Countess of Coningsby and had a succession of titled and noble tenants. It is now a private members club offering style and quietude to its members. A former US Ambassador to the UK, The Hon Raymond G H Seitz, wrote:

'I have witnessed a remarkable concentration of London activity, first in my government role and now again in my private role. London is a cross roads for Europe, the Atlantic and the four corners. So many paths converge in London that it is difficult to keep track of them, to follow the ones you need to or switch over to the ones you want to. Pasley Tyler & Co has planted itself at this busy intersection. Supported by an impressive range of senior and experienced bankers and industrialists, the Pasley Tyler House in Berkeley Square is uniquely designed to provide a private atmosphere from which senior executives can operate efficiently and effectively. It is a sophisticated town house and it fills an important gap.'

Opposite page: Nos 43-46 Berkeley Square.
Right: 42 Berkeley Square.

No 41 now houses the offices of Citigroup. It is sad there is no blue plaque to record the life of one of the most unfortunate fighting admirals of the Napoleonic wars. It is only now in the 21st century that there is talk of a pardon for this man. He engaged a small French fleet off Minorca during the Seven Years' War. The outcome was in some doubt. Admiral Byng was court martialled for failing to engage the enemy properly, he was found guilty and shot. It was a verdict not universally popular even then. This incident prompted Voltaire to write one of his most famous quotations: 'In England, from time to time it is important to kill an Admiral pour encourager les autres.' How strange that along with Clive at No 45, these two such fine 18th-century neighbours should have had such sad ends to their lives.

No 40, with its salmon leaping around a phallic bollard, is a sight to behold and the present 38-36, Berger House is perpendicular in style. To identify this as 'Post World War II blitz economy rebuild' would be entirely wrong. A spectacular great terrace of four elegant houses was razed to the ground making way for Berger House and its neighbour, not too long before the start of World War II. Mr Berger is believed to be the paint manufacturer. Berger House is a testament to commercial success and bad architectural taste.

No 38 was a fine house rivalling No 44 and only slightly less grand, the original plans are available to view in the City of Westminster Archives. The layout of the basement and the attic spaces in particular, chronicle a social history of the time. With kitchen, scullery, butler's pantry, servant's hall, housekeeper's room and those for stewards, valets, maids and chefs, it is possible that a grand house such as this would employ a minimum of 30 people. The first owner was the Duke of Manchester in 1767. He sold it a year later to Robert Child the great banker whose bank, Child's Bank, exists today at No 1 Fleet Street and is now part of the Royal Bank of Scotland. Its connection to the Child family continued for almost exactly 100 years as, after the marriages of Child children to members of the aristocracy it became the home of the Earl of Westmorland and later the Earl of Jersey.

Opposite page, top row: The original No 40 which was occupied by the Duke of Newcastle during the Napoleonic Wars. Next to it, No 40 as it is today.

Opposite page, bottom row: No 38 in 1896 and, next to it, Berger House which now occupies the site.

'George the Third
Ought never to have occurred.
One can only wonder
At so grotesque a blunder.'
'More Biographies', Edmund Clerihew Bentley.

The West End of London has been the home of the Royal Family for more than three centuries. St James's Palace remains the official residence of our Sovereign Lady, Queen Elizabeth, and it was built as such, as long ago as 1531. It is little wonder that through the centuries royalty has been attracted to use and live within the environs of Berkeley Square just a generous stone's throw away. It is of some fascination that the present London home of the head of state was built for a mere duke, indeed the Duke of Buckingham. It was built originally as Arlington House and later immortalised his personal achievements as Buckingham House.

The royal connection with Berkeley Square goes back directly to the Berkeley family. After the death of the 1st Lord Berkeley in 1678 and his firstborn son, the second baron, in 1682, Lady Berkeley with her remaining two sons lived at Berkeley House until 1692 when it was let to Princess Anne of Denmark, later Queen Anne, becoming the last of the Stuart monarchs in 1702. Her marriage to George, Prince of Denmark, a dull man by all accounts, was devoted but unremarkable. She experienced 17 pregnancies between 1683 and 1700 with just five children being born alive and even then the son who outlived infancy failed to survive and inherit the throne. A fussy lady herself she met her match in Lady Berkeley who wasted no time in showing round her distinguished prospective tenant. It is of interest that Princess Anne needed to rent two smaller houses nearby to accommodate her staff and servants. As the Princess left Berkeley House to be accommodated in St James's Palace, Lady Berkeley put the house on the market only to find folk clamouring for its purchase. The Dukes of Devonshire and the Marquis of Normandy (later Duke of Buckingham) found themselves in serious dispute over the purchase. Berkeley House went on to become Devonshire House and the Marquis's house eventually became Buckingham Palace.

It may be a valuable exercise to recall the succession of monarchs since the reign of Charles II. The famous: 'Willie, Willie, Harry, Ste' doggerel proceeds through: Harrys (various), Edwards and Dicks onwards to the first two Queens, Mary and Good Queen Bess, via James I to the two Charles. It is during and after the reign of Charles II that Kings and Queens of the United Kingdom and their families have touched the life and times of Berkeley Square and its surrounds to a greater or lesser degree.

The memory-jogging rhyme identifies these monarchs as:

Charlie two and James again	1660-1685-1688
William and Mary together then	1689-1702
Followed on by Anne o'Gloria	1702-1714
The Georges one two three and four-ia	1714-1727-1760-1820-1830
Then comes William and Victoria	1830-1837-1901
Edward Seven then Georgie Five	1901-1910-1936
Edward George and Liz (alive)	1936-1937-1952

The four Georges reigned from 1714 to 1830 and it could be argued that three of them, certainly, did little to set a high moral tone. They and we were fortunate to have had George III as the longest serving and the most responsible of them all. The kingdom thrived and became one of the greatest empires of the world setting standards of probity and achievement beyond compare.

Meanwhile all the Georges were honoured in one way or another. The parish church built near the Square was named for the Hanover family and George Street bears their name.

The young Georgian royals had a predilection towards marrying for love and/or lust which was not always convenient. The Royal Marriages Act was passed by George III and was designed to allow the Sovereign to have control of the marital destiny of his offspring. Patently it did not work. Both his brothers married commoners morganatically and his son, the Prince of Wales, famously, in secret married Mrs Fitzherbert.

The two most notable residents of this area were the Duke of Clarence and his brother the Duke of Cambridge. Both married commoners. The Duke of Clarence lived in an unpretentious house in Farm Street with his wife, the former Mrs Jordan. The Duke of Cambridge, a great servant of Queen and Country, married the entirely unsuitable Miss Fairbrother, an artiste, no less. The Marriage Act was not invoked; she was called Mrs FitzGeorge and lived comfortably and quietly at No 6 Queens Street. The Duke of Cambridge was a fine field marshal and listed as commander in chief of the Army.

Whilst the two Edwards of the 20th century generally sported themselves in the nightlife of Mayfair it was Edward VIII's brother Albert Duke of York, later George VI, who lived there. Married to Elizabeth Bowes-Lyon, he and his family lived in No 17 Bruton Street, the town house of the Earl and Countess of Strathmore. Here both our present Queen Elizabeth and her sister Princess Margaret were born. It is of some significance that the Home Secretary of the time, Sir William Joynson-Hicks, spent the night in vigil at the birth of Elizabeth, she being third in line to the throne. 17 Bruton Street was razed to the ground even before World War II, giving way to Berkeley Square House.

Below: 17 Bruton Street in 1817.
The house was designed by Isaac Ware and
it became the London home of the Earl
and Countess of Strathmore and, later,
Queen Elizabeth the Queen Mother.

Below right: The Union Flag, flying from
The Naval Club, Hill Street.

BERKELEY SQUARE NORTH SIDE

'Were you with these, my Prince, you'd soon forget,
The pale unripened beauties of the north.'
The Campaign, Joseph Addison.

In the middle of the 18th century, Messrs Cock and Hilliard were developing the Berkeley Estate to the east and west, whilst the north end of the square was part of the Grosvenor Estate. The Berkeleys concentrated upon fine London houses for quality residents, but the Grosvenors saw fit to house those in trade in their portion of the Square. By 1744 there was Hemley's (sometimes Henley's) Coffee House and Francis Hilliard had his house and business sited there as well. In the small space between Jones Street and Davies Street in these early times there were, variously, a hosier, a fruiterer, a shoemaker, a watchmaker and a bookseller.

30 BERKELEY SQUARE

Nos 29 and 30 were both destroyed by German bombs in World War II and the site was rebuilt for the Alcan Company in 1955 by F. G. Minter to the designs of Gunton and Gunton. It was a conventional neo-Georgian office block in red brick. The site was again rebuilt in the 1990s and is the headquarters of GE Corporate Finance. This is a finance company with deep roots in the heavy engineering industry, being derived from General Electric of the United States. With a number of other more modern buildings in the Square, the entrance to this building is a kindly attempt at the inclusion of art within architecture.

28 BERKELEY SQUARE

No 28 was designed and built by Thomas Cubitt. Originally, it was bought by a Henry Powell Collins for £6,500. It is thought to be the work of the bricklayer Alexander Mingay. It is now Morton's, a private members' club of style and discretion.

This page and opposite page: 30 Berkeley Square, the GE building, now occupies the sites of both 29 and 30.

No 27 is thought to be yet another Thomas Cubitt house and built for John Bailey, the owner of Thomas's Hotel next door at No 25. As long ago as 1909 a young architect had designs for a very striking neo classical new building with sharp angular detailing which excited much interest at the Royal Academy. It was but a dream. The house boasts a distinguished role call of owners through the two centuries that include the 8th Duke of Beaufort and the 5th Earl of Airlie. More infamously, among those who live there, Edwin John James QC MP was the first ever QC to be disbarred, and was described at the time as 'this infamous pre-eminence'. He emigrated to the United States and quite possibly died there in a gentle sulk.

It was under the stewardship of Mrs Sainsbury-Jones during World War I that the house distinguished itself as a temporary hospital. The Army Council awarded a certificate, now cast in bronze and displayed as a plaque on the front of the house. This plaque states, under the Royal Coat of Arms:

During the Great War of 1914-1919 (sic)

this building was a hospital for British sick and wounded = The Army Council in the name of the Nation thank those who have rendered to this valuable and patriotic assistance in the hour of its emergency and they desire also to express their deep appreciation of the wholehearted attention which the staff of this hospital gave to the patients who were under their care = The war has once again called upon the devotion and self sacrifice of British men and women and the Nation will remember with pride and gratitude their willing and inestimable service. This certificate is presented by the Army Council as a permanent record of their thanks = to be placed in the building which has been known and used as Mrs Sainsbury-Jones' Hospital for Officers 27 Berkeley Square W1 Hospital for British Sick and Wounded during the Great War 1914-1919.

Signed Louis Frood Churchill. The War Office London 1920.

The first dwellings on this site were numbered 28 and 29 Berkeley Square and included a farrier's shop established in 1755 in the Grosvenor Estate. They remained workshops for artisans until early into the following century. The farrier, a Francis Cornish, later sold his premises to William Linnell who with his son John established a reputation as being amongst the most important cabinetmakers and upholsterers of the 18th century. One of the more eccentric later occupants of this site was Gregory William Eardley-Twistleton-Fiennes, 8th Baron Saye and Sele (1769-1884) who is said to be the only man to have consumed an omelette of golden pheasant eggs. One night as he was going out to dinner, his butler asked for instructions regarding his return. They were: 'Place two bottles of sherry by my bedside, and wake me the day after tomorrow.'

In 1795 most famously it became the site of Thomas's Hotel, also known as Bailey's Hotel, after John Bailey one of its original proprietors. In its heyday, Thomas's wined, dined and accommodated the world of rank and fashion in great number. They included Lord Ruthven, Viscount Midleton, The Earl of Kintore, the Duke of Atholl, the Earl of Coventry, Sir Henry Des Voeux, Lord Bolton and many, many more.

This was to last for almost another century. In 1905, Thomas's Hotel, very much outdated by competition from newer hotels like Claridge's and the Savoy, was replaced by the present apartment building. One of the earliest residents was Jimmy Buchanan, well-known, wealthy man about town. In 1922 he was approached by Maundy Gregory, Lloyd George's honours broker, with the offer of a title in return for a large donation to the Liberal Party. Fascinated by this, but distrusting Gregory, he was careful to sign the cheque using his proposed title 'Baron Woolavington' which he duly acquired. For many years post-war, No 25 was chiefly occupied by Reader's Digest Association Ltd, later on becoming the offices of Cadbury Schweppes plc.

24 AND 23 BERKELEY SQUARE

Even the most intense research reveals nothing on these two properties other than No 23, on the corner of Bruton Place and Berkeley Square, was redeveloped by Gale Stephen Steiner. Both are now offices.

'But now ye wait at Heaven's Gate and not in Berkeley Square.'
'Tommy', Rudyard Kipling.

It is just possible that God looked down upon Berkeley Square during its creation and, seeing it placed securely in the hands of Lady Berkeley of Stratton, he saw that it was good. With so many other things requiring his attention at the time, such as a philandering monarch and warring nations, it is just possible that he left the square to its own devices. The Church of England appeared to be happy to leave it to the landowners to provide places of worship for the people. It was not to be disappointed, as a number of proprietary chapels were established.

The established parish church was St George's Hanover Square. It was hardly within a reasonable Sunday's strolling distance available for all the 18th and 19th-century wealthy, God-fearing folk of Mayfair. The Grosvenor and Berkeley Estates were within the parish of St George's in Hanover Square, quite an exhausting sedan car ride away. Sir Richard Grosvenor responded to his perceived responsibilities very early on. He built the Grosvenor Chapel in South Audley Street, which survives to this day. Built in 1730, it is a most elegant structure of simple design. Clearly the Grosvenors cared for the spiritual welfare of their tenants and leaseholders in a way that the Berkeleys took a little while to replicate. The Grosvenor Chapel appears to have been a private chapel for the first 99 years until its original lease ran out. It was then embraced within the Parish of St George's as a chapel of ease. Slowly through the next century it acquired all the facilities and licences to take on the full range of offices of the Church of England. Sir John Betjeman prayed there; perhaps it was this bell that summoned him and there is a plaque commemorating the large numbers of American servicemen and women who found peace and succour there during the World War II.

The Berkeley family eventually accepted their responsibilities and a little later, in 1750, built the Berkeley Chapel on the corner of John Street (now Chesterfield Gardens) and Charles Street. It was a fine building with a Doric porch and a cupola. After a colourful history of eccentric pastors and equally eccentric congregations, a reportedly small and smelly, over upholstered chapel was demolished in 1907.

Most notorious of the Mayfair chapels was the Curzon Chapel also built around 1730. It was situated in Curzon Street just opposite Crewe House and run by an enterprising minister who took full advantage of a need to pay due respect to both God and Mammon. The chapel was run as a strict business providing lawful marriages to those in need of such a sacrament with few if any questions asked. Licences, reading of banns and parental consent were courtesies deemed unnecessary. Dr Alexander Keith would happily marry those off the street at a guinea a wedding. It was good business and the rewards went straight into his pocket. Dr Keith did not endear himself to his parent parish church of St George and, in 1742, the rector chose to ex-communicate him, hoping to deprive him of the living. That was not the end of the story. Though sentenced to jail in Fleet Prison, Dr Keith contrived to ex-communicate the rector of the parish and his bishop and, in passing, continued to conduct marriage services through agents in a house two doors from the original Mayfair Chapel. What initiative!

The church in Farm Street is the only real church within the Berkeley Square Estate, being 'The Church of the Immaculate Conception'. It has the ability to surprise those who care to step through the small side door of an impressively large front door. From the street, it is baroque and business-like with the frontage of a town house. Once inside it has the breathtaking dimensions of a Tardis: to use a totally inappropriate *Dr Who* metaphor. The high altar appears to have stepped out of Rome with its huge stained glass window casting rainbows of bright light into the nave. The Stations of the Cross are carved and crafted with such great competence as they settle back between brightly painted statues of saints along the wall at the side. It was built in the 1840s as the work of the architect J J Scoles. One needs to view it from Mount Street Garden at the rear of the church to see his cleverly engineered horizontal flying buttresses supporting the neighbouring vaulted ceilings.

In Curzon Street is the Third Church of Christ Scientist. Christian Science is a young church that appears to have started in Scotland in the 1900s and known as the First Church. A splinter church called the Second Church broke away as did a further one, called simply the Third Church of Christ Scientist. The impressive doorway is at 9 Curzon Street and offers a view of a well-kept courtyard garden surrounded by functional office accommodation.

Page 90: The Church of the Immaculate Conception, Farm Street.

Opposite page, top left: Mayfair Chapel (or Curzon Chapel), about 1740.

Opposite page, bottom left: Courtyard of the Third Church of Christ Scientist.

Opposite page, right: Third Church of Christ Scientist.

BERKELEY SQUARE EAST SIDE

The east side of the square was the first to be developed in terms of housing. Lady Berkeley's provisions for a square and later Lord Devonshire's determination to preserve the view from his house, were being honoured. The road, upon which the first houses on the Square to the east were built, was originally called New Berkeley Street for a very brief period of time and later called Berkeley Row which also applied to the north side.

However, the east side, and that of the south, were to feel the wind of change, which arose from the demolition of Devonshire House in 1924 and the rapid rise of New Devonshire House in 1925. Headlines in *The Evening News*, 21 July 1930, proclaimed: 'Fifteen Famous Mayfair Mansions In The Market', with the sub heading: 'Mansion Flats instead of Mansions'. It was the start of a property boom led by Canadian Pacific Railways as they optimised their new 98-year lease with plans to build what was to be the largest office building in Europe.

At about the same time the buildings between Bruton Street and Bruton Place (what were Nos 20, 21 and 22) on Berkeley Square were also requisitioned for development, though on a less grand scale.

Berkeley Square House now stands on the site of 20 houses of historical interest, some of which were on Berkeley Square itself (Nos 11 to 19). In its time, and up until the 1950s, it was considered one of the largest blocks of shops and offices in Europe. It was presumably perceived as being a showpiece of modern architecture. Today, whilst probably undermining the reputation of grace and elegance bestowed by earlier centuries, it remains a much sought-after address from which to operate a business. Of interest is the fact that in the 1930s, Lord Bearsted sold the greater share of the property to Canadian Pacific Railway Company who proposed to erect a grand hotel. This was abandoned because of the depression in the early Thirties. Berkeley Square House cost around £2,000,000 to build. The great coup seemed to be that of an unlikely cigar-smoking American, Malcolm MacKenzie, a recent partner of Knight Frank & Rutley. He appeared to have lived with the project from 1930 and saw it as one of his greatest achievements to have let the whole property to the relatively newly created Air Ministry.

Page 95: The houses on the corner of Bruton Street and Berkeley Square, by Pitts 1938.

City of Westminster Archives Centre.

Above and opposite page, left: Two illustrations specially drawn for 'The Sunday Times'
by Hanslip Fletcher, 1930.
The captions at the time read: 'The changing character of London is, perhaps, nowhere more
strikingly seen than in the commercialisation of Mayfair. Residencies in Bruton Street and
Berkeley Square are soon to be demolished to make way for business premises.'
City of Westminster Archives Centre.

*Below: Another view of the houses soon
to be demolished.*

*Top right: A photograph of No 21,
taken in 1930.*

Bottom right: Demolition starts in 1938.

20 BERKELEY SQUARE

No 20 was once the home of Colley Cibber. His was a name to be conjured with in 1753. A distinguished actor and dramatist when the profession was more one of doubt rather than respectability, he attracted great respect in his time. He was born at Southwark, the son of Caius Gabriel Cibber, a Danish sculptor, and his second wife Jane Colley, an heiress. The Colleys came from Rutland and Colley was sent to school in Grantham where he displayed: 'a special sharpness of intellect and aptitude for verse writing which gained him consideration from his masters, and a conceit which rendered him unpopular with his fellows'. His mother was held to enjoy descent from William of Wykeham, but his application for entry to Winchester College was unsuccessful. Having directed his attention to the theatre and stage, he was later made Poet Laureate in 1730.

21 BERKELEY SQUARE

Next door to the Cibber family lived Lady Anne Barnard who is famous for writing the song 'Auld Robin Gray'. How fickle is such fame when of course the only song that cries aloud this location is that of the nightingale.

'Oh sair did we greet and mickle did we say,
We took but ae kiss and we tore ourselves away.
I wish I were dead, but I'm not like to die,
And why do I live to say, waes me!'

A tale of a sailor home from the seas to find his girlfriend a-marrying Auld Robin Gray! Anne Barnard, a well-connected lady of Barnard Castle fame, approached the status of a literary giant in her day.

Top right: Office and retail building on the site of 20-22 Berkeley Square.

19 BERKELEY SQUARE

Gazing through the window of Jack Barclay's on the corner of Bruton Street and dreaming of owning one of the finest horseless carriages for sale in the polished showroom, one could be forgiven for indulging in more strange flights of fancy. In this particular corner of the Square, an apothecary plied his trade in the 18th century. It is likely he was a Samuel Despaignol who was also a surgeon and medical practitioner. Whilst a co-founder of St George's Hospital, he set up his own local health service and, for a retainer of £50 per annum from the parish, he, in return did: 'take care of and administer Physick to the poor of the parish and act as parish apothecary': a noble response to his calling.

13 BERKELEY SQUARE

Edward Bouverie who planted the plane trees we see today in Berkeley Square, lived in this house. He was the fourth child of William de Bouverie, the first Earl of Radnor.

*Below: The advertisement for the sale of the site
that became Berkeley Square House.
'The Times' 24 July 1936.
City of Westminster Archives Centre.*

12 BERKELEY SQUARE

No 12 was a house with naval connections. Built for 'Foul Weather Jack' Admiral Sir John Norris, it was acquired by the 3rd Earl of Albemarle, whose brother, Admiral the Honourable Augustus Keppel, also used the house when in London. He was one of a band of Admiral Politicians, a quite common practice in the 18th century. The Albemarle family name of Keppel is also closely connected with King Edward VII. However there is no evidence to suggest that his liaison with Alice Keppel had any connection with Berkeley Square.

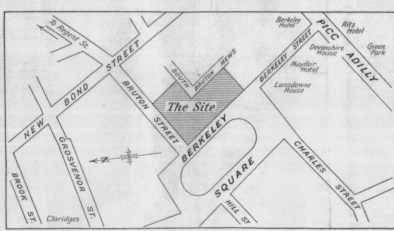

26   **The Times**   THURSDAY, JULY 24, 1930

LONDON: 20, HANOVER-SQUARE, W.1.
Telephone: Mayfair 3066.
EDINBURGH: 90, PRINCES-STREET.
ASHFORD, KENT: 41, BANK-STREET,

KNIGHT, FRANK & RUTLEY.

FOUNDLING ESTATE OFFICE:
11-12, GRENVILLE-STREET, W.C.1.
RICHINGS PARK ESTATE, IVER, BUCKS,
AND 298, REGENT-STREET, W.1.
WELWYN GARDEN CITY: BRIDGE-ROAD.

BY AUCTION ON 25TH SEPTEMBER NEXT.

MAYFAIR

BERKELEY SQUARE & BRUTON STREET

ADJOINING BOND-STREET AND PICCADILLY

THE FINEST AVAILABLE SITE IN THE WEST END OF LONDON

THE SITE IS

IMMEDIATELY AVAILABLE

FOR THE ERECTION OF

ONE OF THE MOST IMPORTANT

HOTEL

FLAT

OR

BUSINESS BUILDINGS

IN

LONDON

WITH SHOPS

ON THE GROUND FLOOR

THE SITE OCCUPIES

AN UNRIVALLED SITUATION

OVERLOOKING

LONDON'S MOST CENTRAL

AND

BEAUTIFUL SQUARE

IN THE HEART OF

THE FASHIONABLE SHOPPING
CENTRE

WITH W. AND W.S.W. ASPECT

AND COMPRISES

Nos. 11, 12, 13, 14, 15, 16, 17, 18 & 19,
BERKELEY SQUARE

Nos. 15, 16, 17, 18, 19 & 20,
BRUTON STREET

AREA 55,000 SQUARE FEET

HIGHLY VALUABLE SHOPPING FRONTAGES
OF 542 FEET

THE BUILDING LEASE FOR 99 YEARS

AT A NOMINAL GROUND-RENT OF £5,800 PER ANNUM.

WILL BE OFFERED WITH POSSESSION UNLESS PREVIOUSLY SOLD PRIVATELY

AT THE HANOVER SQUARE ESTATE ROOMS.

SOLICITORS:
MESSRS. BURTON & RAMSDEN,
30, CLARGES STREET,
LONDON, W.1.

SURVEYORS:
MESSRS. WILSON & CO.,
14, MOUNT STREET, W.1.

AUCTIONEERS:
MESSRS. KNIGHT, FRANK & RUTLEY,
20, HANOVER SQUARE, W.1.

11 BERKELEY SQUARE

In 1771, Horace Walpole came to live at 11 Berkeley Square for the last 15 years of his life. He is reported as saying: 'I came to town today to take possession of Berkeley Square and am well pleased with my habitation as I can with anything at present.' He was the 4th Earl of Orford, son of Sir Robert Walpole, the Prime Minister and at one time a Member of Parliament. He was a prolific writer and author. In 1747 Walpole acquired Strawberry Hill in Twickenham, which was remodelled in the new Gothick style, with plasterwork in pastel shades. He was a man of letters, a very popular houseguest in Berkeley Square in earlier days but he died reclusively of cold and gout.

Top left and above: Contemporary sketches of the demolition sites.

Top right: The corner of Berkeley Square with Bruton Street. The photograph carried the note, 'A familiar view that has vanished forever'.

Opposite page: Berkeley Square east, by Pitts, 1937.
Houses before demolition to make way for
Berkeley Square House.
City of Westminster Archives Centre.

Above: A similar view at the turn of the 19th century.

Opposite page: Berkeley Square east, 1926. Houses before demolition to make way for Berkeley Square House.

Mary Evans Picture Library.

Above: The same view today.

Top left and opposite page: The stunning entrance of Berkeley Square House, which in 1937 was considered to be a great positive architectural statement in terms of size, style and quality.

Below left: The minimalist interior decor of the corridors which provide access to the spacious office accommodation.

Below right: A view of the entrance from above.

Opposite, this page and overleaf:
Artists impressions for the Berkeley Square
House opening ceremony brochure of 1937.

Opposite page: Note the total lack of adherence
to a proper scale. People and cars are
diminished in size and it is amusing to note
how very broad the road is shown. There is no
indication of either pavement or the Square
itself. Also of interest are the original houses
illustrated to the left of the picture. These were
next to be developed and were soon demolished.

Right: A different view, showing Hill Street and
the houses on the west side, opposite Berkeley
Square House.

PHANTOMS AND APPARITIONS

No account of Berkeley Square and the environs is complete without a discussion of the vivid tales of the various ghosts and apparitions that have been handed down through the centuries. Perhaps No 50 should be left to last with its reputation of being the most haunted house in London. It is just possible that it is a national, if not international, accolade.

There are approximately 30 firm records of paranormal visitation within the postal area of W1 London, many of them associated with the houses and streets close to Berkeley Square.

Before Fitzmaurice Street became a thoroughfare and before the old Lansdowne House became the Lansdowne Club, there was an alleyway linking Berkeley Square with Curzon Street. This was known as Lansdowne Passage. It boasted a central bollard to prevent highwaymen from riding through to escape the law. Here, footpads and shadowy figures are said to appear as the ghosts of those who fled the law in the 19th century.

A greater drama lay in Hill Street where the evil and thoroughly lecherous Lord Lyttelton lived. He must have rued the day he seduced the two daughters (some say three), of a Mrs Amphlett. It is said that a woman in white, and by common consent identified as the aggrieved Mrs Amphlett herself, appeared at the roué's bedside telling him he was to die. He thought he could bargain with her, asking how many months he had left, and she replied three days. He dismissed her warning and left with his valet for his country house in Epsom (Pit Place) and, on the third day when undressing for bed, he simply collapsed and died. History does not relate whether he would have been forgiven for the seduction of one daughter though there is a simple message in that it proved to be a dangerous move to cross Mrs Amphlett. Lord Lyttelton was, besides his being prone to the occasional dalliance, a brave man. He tried not simply to exorcise, but completely destroy the ghost of 50 Berkeley Square with a blunderbuss.

At No 25 Brook Street, not too far from Berkeley Square, in the house once occupied by George Frederic Handel, a woman's presence is marked curiously by the smell of perfume. Lacking a true sense of belonging, she also haunts the house next door. Some may raise an eyebrow at the reliability of this evidence by none other than Jimi Hendrix, who saw her in the 1960s. This ghost was exorcised in July 2001 and there is no more to say.

The story of 53 Berkeley Square is yet another spooky tale. Apparently an old man was seen staring with a glazed look from the window of this house and, the report goes on, this 17th century gentleman's daughter eloped against his wishes and it is with heavy heart that he awaited her return. It is probably the least chilling of all ghost stories and may have been confused with a sad story of love's labours and ambitions being lost further up the road.

A certain Mr Myers of distinguished lineage bought No 50 cheaply in the latter half of the 19th century because it had been left empty for a number of years. It had already acquired a reputation for being haunted. Having gone to considerable lengths to prepare this fine house for his bride with equally fine furniture, furnishings and maidservants, Myers was shunned. Jilted at the last moment the young woman married someone else. He was so shocked and broken hearted that he never left the house again and went mad. He employed a housekeeping couple who were as reclusive as he was and, when he died, all that he had bought to impress the young bride that was never to be, was found wrapped and stowed, unpacked, in the original crates and boxes. His only friend and visitor was his sister to whom he left the house, but she took no interest in the property. It remained in decay until at least 1880. However sad this particular 19th century story, it cannot be responsible solely for the whole range and variety of reports on ghosts and apparitions attributed to this house. Mr Myers is said to be sitting, forlorn at his window and waiting.

Other ghosts of No 50 were, variously, ghastly horrific apparitions of shapeless and slimy forms making gruesome slopping noises and with gaping and frightening jaws. Equally there was more than one presence, be it the noise of heavy objects being moved, bells that rang, lights appearing at night in different rooms or the groans of a seriously unhappy spirit. In addition, the very walls were charged with electric terror. A maid died of fright when sleeping in an upstairs room; it is this room that is the most dreadful and horrifying haunted room in the whole of Christendom. Adeline, a coy wife from the 18th century, hung screaming from the window of an upper room in an attempt to flee from the carnal advances of no less a man than her husband. A wee Scottish lass, dressed in a kilt, was claimed to be tortured and frightened by a wicked Dickensian nanny. She roams the rooms at night wringing her hands and sobbing. There is another sobbing female, a woman who left her husband for another man and afterwards thoroughly regretted it all. Elegantly dressed, she haunts like a model for a Tissot masterpiece: wide brimmed hat, white blouse with a high collar and puffed, ham bone sleeves together with a long black bustled skirt. Without doubt she is the most elegant of ghosts. There is yet one more. A Mr Dupré locked his mad brother in an upstairs room and fed him through a hole in the door; no wonder his brother was mad.

Then there were the ghost busters. Sir Robert Warboys arranged to sleep in the room with friends below in the servants' quarters. His distress signal was to ring the servants' bell. By the time he had rung the bell twice, his friends found him dead. Lord Lyttelton of Hill Street took time off from seducing young maidens to repeat the Warboys experiment. He took two loaded blunderbuss weapons with him. He survived the night but not before discharging one gun at a strange apparition. However, as reported elsewhere in these pages, he was victim to the wrath of another ghost. One cannot be certain that there is an end to these stories. However the last recorded paranormal incident took place whilst the house was empty and in the ownership of Mr Meyer's sister. Two sailors on a run ashore in London, like many a matelot before and since, found themselves a little the worse for wear from having overindulged of London's strong ale. They had no money and nowhere to rest their befuddled heads in a big city. They discovered No 50 empty and broke in, seeking shelter for the night. The story is that the ghost appeared, causing one sailor to flee and the other to jump out of the window and impale himself on the railings below. There are no reports on how this evidence was received at any subsequent inquiry.

The Earl of Selkirk bought 50 Berkeley Square in 1880, untroubled by all the stories of the past, and the house was restored and the ghosts quietly retreated. The present tenants Maggs Bros and the many who work and have worked there over the last 50 years or so, remain unruffled and untroubled.

One further ghost is reported to inhabit the Clermont Club at No 44. Lady Finch's major-domo has chosen to linger on in spirit form and, over the last 200 years, his ghost, resplendent in smart green uniform and handsome periwig, has often been seen flitting up and down the grand staircase, keeping a watchful eye on the playing of roulette and backgammon that now goes on in the grand salon. He is said to walk with a slight limp, and his appearances are brief for, having satisfied himself that all is well, he melts through one of the staircase doors and ascends the narrow, spiral staircase to his bedroom at the top of the house.

*Berkeley Square south side 1860. Unnamed
artist. The gateway in the wall to the left was
the entrance to the original Lansdowne House.*
Mary Evans Picture Library.

116

'Prison'd in a parlour snug and small,
Like bottle wasps upon a southern wall.'
'Retirement', William Cowper.

For nearly three centuries, up to the 1930s, the southern boundary of Berkeley Square was the garden wall of the great Lansdowne House. This was to be the first of three buildings to carry the name. The very first Lansdowne House, originally called Bute House, was started by John Stuart the 3rd Earl of Bute. Hugely influential, though not universally popular, the Earl rose in rank and influence. By 1761 he was the King's First Minister, with homes in Scotland, Kenwood House in north London and a rented town house in Audley Street. Not satisfied with this, he needed a magnificent mansion close to government and close to his mistress, the widow of Frederick, Prince of Wales. The 5th and last Lord Berkeley, grandson of a prudent and shrewd grandmother, the 1st and only Lady Berkeley of Stratton, sold two portions of land to the Earl of Bute for the princely sum of £115. Bute employed Robert Adam to design and build for him a palace with gardens stretching across those of Devonshire House to the south. This was not a happy time as there was little trust between Adam and his client. Just four years later, by 1765, Lord Bute tired of his London house project and sold the unfinished building and site to Lord Shelbourne who, by 1784, had become the Marquess of Lansdowne.

Thus Shelburne House, later Lansdowne House, was completed and set to remain in that family for five generations and was witness throughout to moments of great history. Early on, in 1782, the treaty bringing to an end the American War of Independence was drafted in one of its rooms. In 1834 both Houses of Parliament were destroyed by fire, and for some years after, its dining room was used for Privy Council meetings and in 1902-04 the 5th Marquess, as Foreign Secretary, negotiated the Entente Cordiale and the Anglo-Japanese Treaty. No longer in constant use by the family, it became a first-aid station during World War I and remaining with the family until 1921 when it was let. Probably its most distinguished tenant was Harry Gordon Selfridge, the flamboyant American department store pioneer. He managed to set tongues wagging after installing the improbable and sometime be-feathered Dolly Sisters, Hungarian cabaret artists, as house guests.

The original Lansdowne House survived until the 1930s and during this period a new class of industrialist was beginning to emerge. It was the genesis of the property developer. Already Devonshire House had been razed to the ground and replaced by office, retail and hotel accommodation and work had begun on Berkeley Square House. There was a growing need to create higher-density residential occupation and office space in the capitals of the world. New York's skyscraper philosophy was gaining a foothold in London. In Britain it was the era of the semi-detached house and the steel 'Crittall' window frames. The fine Georgian architects and the builders Messrs Cock and Hillyard and their kind must have turned in their graves as a second Lansdowne House rose with great ordinariness. It was red brick and mean, containing flats, offices and shops. During World War II, it was requisitioned by the Air Ministry. One claim to fame was that Johnny Weissmuller of *Tarzan* fame had a flat there.

Old Lansdowne House which, with its gardens, occupied the whole of the south side. Owing to restrictions imposed by the 1st Lady Berkeley of Stratton, the mansion faced Hay Hill and not Berkeley Square.

The Lansdowne Club, Fitzmaurice Place. This is the original facade of old Lansdowne House, moved during redevelopment in the 1930s, to join with the original rear rooms of the house. Rooms of the middle section were shipped to a museum in the USA.

The new Lansdowne House closed off the southern side of Berkeley Square replacing the old garden wall. The other part of the project was the redevelopment of the first Lansdowne House. The Bruton Club had bought the old house and, whilst alarm bells rang and there was talk of architectural rape, the process of converting the old Lansdowne House into the Lansdowne Club was a matter blessed with considerable inspiration. The biggest feat was to remove the front of the building that extended far across what is now Fitzmaurice Street and to move and join it to the rear portion which retained the original sculpture gallery and the entrance hall. In the meantime, however, the drawing room and dining room were transported to Philadelphia and preserved in their Museum of Art.

The Lansdowne Club in Fitzmaurice Place now completes the circuit of Berkeley Square. It remains an impressive building with its facade a superb example of its Georgian heritage, allowing this to be the most sensitive of all the pre-war developments in the Square. Internally just the ballroom and a small number of other rooms and anterooms cling to their heritage. The larger component, particularly the 'club' accommodation and facilities, were built in the art deco 'ocean liner' fashion of the time.

Fitzmaurice Place now links the Square with Curzon Street and was until recent times a cul-de-sac built, in 1935, to service the doorways of the Lansdowne Club. Earlier the sinister Lansdowne Steps which traced the boundary between Devonshire House and Lansdowne House, was the quickest route from the southwest corner of the Square and survived to the 1960s.

Lansdowne Row separates the modern Lansdowne House from the Mayfair Hotel. It is a foot passage with a modest range of shops and pavement cafés and has little relationship with the up-market grandeur of the rest of the estate. There is always an air of fun and purpose as people come out to fortify themselves with nicotine and caffeine, to purchase modest essentials or simply to sit and enjoy a meal and watch the world go by.

Right: The third, and present, Lansdowne House, designed by the architects, Chapman Taylor Partners.

The present Lansdowne House is the third to bear the name. In the 1980s, the site owners Legal and General were granted planning permission for a building design that impressed the inspectors, who reported the proposed design as innovative and providing a building of excellence. This was great praise from such a traditionally undemonstrative body. The architects, Chapman Taylor Partners, were determined to include style and elegance. The design incorporated three tiers of offices over seven floors surrounding an atrium containing tall exotic bamboos plants in water cascades and friendly bronze flamingos. It should be said that the sponsors and architects appeared thrilled, excited and proud of their achievement as the building was opened, proclaiming: 'The new Lansdowne House will carry its illustrious name into the next century as a worthy and distinguished companion to the remaining historic houses that have graced Berkeley Square for the last 200 years.'

This extract from the architect's description demonstrates their enthusiasm: 'The external elevations are clad in Whitbed Portland Stone, with a textured and rusticated base in Hantergantick Cornish Grey Granite. The use of Blue Bahia granite for the head and sill stones to the showcase windows of the ground floor retail units is intended to highlight the strongly modelled lower stages and with the help of precisely carved decorative geometric patterns, add interest and colour at pedestrian level.'

Whilst in many ways spectacular, with unrestrained usage of patterned granites and marbles from all over the world, the building seems to acquire a functional modesty as it quietly contains the businesses therein.

Left: The second Lansdowne House (1935-1985).

Opposite page: The atrium of the present, third, Lansdowne House.

Photographs courtesy of Chapman Taylor Partners.

St Mary-Le-'Bourne'

Mary-Le-'Bourne Lane

The Monk's Pool

Rasputin

Gallow's Pool

Sweeney Todd

The Fishing Hut

Tyburn Road

Brook Street

Grosvenor Street

Gobio Glide

Fry

Berkeley Water
Meadows
Newt Colony

The Coursing Pool

The Tyburn Beagles

St James's Square Beagles

Boundary Line'

The Smoke House'

Hare's Ear

The Long Drop

The New
Fishing Hut

The Flyfishers Club
69 Brook Street

The Jezzabelle

The Sheep Dip

Cowford

Rat's Tailed
Nymph

Mrs Palmer

Brown Emerger
(On the Dropper)

Tup's Indispensable

Piccadilly

Suspender

Whiskey Fly

The Nymphette's Swim

Jersey Herd
Regal Outlet

Stimulator

Effluvius Pool

Grizzly King

King's Scholars Pond

Chomper

Salmon Ladder

Victoria Street

Wooly Bugger

Rodent's
Retreat

The River Tyburn
The Tyburn Angling Society
Est. 1399

Raking for Gudgeon on
the long drop opposite'
the Fishing Hut.

Merkin Muddler

Rat-Faced
McDougal

The Spies Pool

Bow Ditch

Mole Nymph

Cavent Gobio Gobio

RIVER THAMES

Vauxhall Bridge

Simon Trinneal '99

124

THE RIVER TYBURN

'Runs not a river by my palace wall?
Have I not sacks to sew up wives withal?'
'The Rose and the Ring', William Makepeace Thackery.

Often confused with the Tyburn Brook, which runs past the place of execution, the Tyburn was originally called the Teo Burns (Two Brooks), and was first referred to in a Royal Charter of AD 959. The river rises on Haverstock Hill in Hampstead, and flows through the valley between Primrose Hill and Ordnance Hill, across Prince Albert Gate and over the Grand Union Canal in a cast-iron pipe built within the brick foot bridge, continuing its journey south to the Thames at Vauxhall, via Regent's Park and St James's Park. It is a stream in London, which now runs to meet the River Thames at Pimlico through a great arch in the riverbank called the Kingschoole Sluice, near Vauxhall Bridge. The River Tyburn is one of some 13 of London's hidden rivers and streams, the Fleet and the Westbourne being another two. From the 13th century, the Tyburn supplied water for London via elm trunk channels that were later changed to leather pipes. As London gradually developed into the city we know today, so the length of the Tyburn River became completely enclosed in culverts and underground conduits over its entire length. Needless to say, one such channel gave its name to Conduit Street just off New Bond Street.

There is still one place where the clean and running water of the Tyburn can be seen and that is beneath the basement of Grays Mews, home of Grays Antiques just off Oxford Street, where at one time there was a pool with golden fish. The river's name has gained much notoriety being the same as the site of the Tyburn Tree, the triangulated gallows permanently erected close to what is now Marble Arch, and enduring until the 18th century. Oxford Street was known as Tyburn Road and Park Lane was Tyburn Lane. Brook Street in Mayfair takes its name from the Tyburn, which at one time was referred to as the Tyburn Brook though there is confusion as this name referred to another north London stream. Having in early times contributed to the provision of fresh water to the city, it is now a component of London's sewage system.

The presence of the river has made an indelible imprint upon the map of London. Whilst paving and closure hide its waters from view, its very presence dislocated the Georgians' plans for a square grid development of the West End of London. Drunken loops of pathways followed by diagonals of connecting streets are witness to the compromises made to incorporate this natural feature. To this day the river tumbles gently and silently beneath Marylebone Lane across Oxford Street, then proceeding down Molton Lane at an angle as it defines the triangular shape of the mews building, which is Grays Antiques. It flows on beneath Avery Row, southeasterly, before changing course to the southwest just missing the relatively new Time Life building on New Bond Street, Bruton Street intersection. Flowing onwards to Berkeley Square it is covered by Bruton Lane and then most curiously, instead of cooling the feet of those who take their coffee at the pavement tables of Lansdowne Row, it curves violently north in an ox bow lake gesture nodding to Lansdowne House in an endeavour to nourish the flowers at the earlier site of the flowershop of Miss Moyeses and Mr Stevens. Then, just touching Curzon Street, it whisks off south under Green Park eventually to disgorge its somewhat unsavoury waters into the Thames.

THE FIRST FISH OF THE SPRING RUN !

Illustration on this page and pages 124, 127 and 129, courtesy of The Tyburn Angling Society.

The Monks' Pool

Tyburn Bridge

The Gallows Pool

The Fishing Hut

The New Fishing Hut

Footbridge

The Master's Office

Bruton Bridge

The Jezebel

Footbridge

Nymphettes Swim

Piccadilly Bridge

The Sheep Dip

Not well known is the Tyburn Angling Society whose activities centre upon the restoration of the River Tyburn to its former glory of an open river running through metropolitan London. With its president the Hon Nicholas Soames MP and the triturus (pertaining to newts) warden, former London Mayor Ken Livingstone, it could well represent a powerful lobby. Clearly a great deal of property would need to be demolished, to say the very least. Plans suggest the first phase would be to demolish South Molton Street followed by cutting a swathe through Green Park and of course demolishing Buckingham Palace.

In May 2002 the publication *Property Week* was able to claim what can only be described as a scoop, headlined:

'LANDOWNERS WILL HAND OVER THEIR TITLE DEEDS IN EXCHANGE FOR A PLAQUE ON A PARK BENCH, OR A NAMED POOL IN ONE OF THE RIVER'S MANY MEANDERS.

'*Property Week* can exclusively reveal shocking plans set to change the face of the capital. "Comfortably, £1bn worth of property is set to go," reveals the honorary secretary of the Tyburn Angling Society, the ancient and secretive group behind controversial plans to restore the River Tyburn to street level. The first phase will see the demolition of trendy South Molton Street, Grosvenor Estates' new headquarters and much of the Berkeley Square estate as the Tyburn is reborn. Later phases will include cutting a swathe through Green Park and demolishing Buckingham Palace. "Our research suggests that prior to its misappropriation by the city in 1236 the Tyburn was once the dominant flow (in what is now known as the Thames Valley)," claims the secretary.

'In a bid to return the Tyburn to its pre-18th century glory, the society will be forced to demolish a number of properties above the river, which currently runs below ground from Marylebone to Vauxhall Bridge. In its heyday, the Tyburn supported some of London's best salmon fishing and provided cooking water to the burgeoning financial centre, but today it lies neglected below the streets of Mayfair.

'A *Property Week* investigation has revealed that the society's routes go back as far as a royal charter in AD 959. In a complex funding arrangement that has set tongues wagging in the City, the Tyburn Angling Society proposes a "swap". In layman's terms, landowners will hand over the title deeds to their properties in exchange for a plaque on a bench, a dedicated tree or even a named pool in one of the river's many meanderings.

'It is also believed that the society will be seeking reverse rights-of-light compensation from the owners of buildings that are improved by the development. Just as buildings whose views might be obscured by a development are entitled to compensation, so those whose view will be improved are expected to be asked for contributions to part-fund the plans. Sources indicate that supportive landowners may be given riparian fishing rights. Agents also report that buildings not earmarked for demolition and fronting the Tyburn should see substantial rental growth in coming years.'

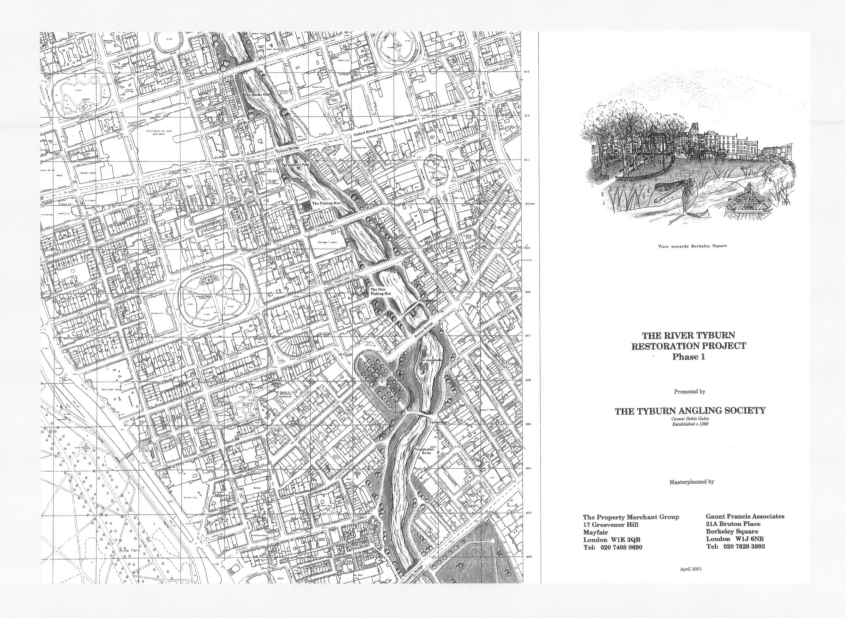

View towards Berkeley Square

**THE RIVER TYBURN
RESTORATION PROJECT
Phase 1**

Promoted by

THE TYBURN ANGLING SOCIETY

*Caveat Gobio Gobio
Established c.1399*

Masterplanned by

The Property Merchant Group
17 Grosvenor Hill
Mayfair
London W1K 3QB
Tel: 020 7408 0690

Gaunt Francis Associates
21A Bruton Place
Berkeley Square
London W1J 6NB
Tel: 020 7629 3993

April 2001

It can be revealed that the society's secret headquarters are in Great Portland Street with every member having a distinctive role. A majority of specific responsibilities for officers of the society reflect the present purpose of the river, being incorporated in London's sewage system. Latrine orderlies of varying degrees of qualification swell their numbers, mingling with volestranglers, narglers pursuivant, sommeliers, choirmasters and custodians of tools (entrenching). If nothing else these worthies have much patience and not a little sense of humour.

THE EASTERN ESTATE

'The east is a career.'
'Tankred', Benjamin Disraeli.

It is strange to consider that many of the small shops in the whole of London were built primarily as residences. Home owners might well have identified that their best prospect for family security was to enter into trade. It is significant in Berkeley Square and the streets around, that, for some reason, houses towards the east became commercialised whilst those to the west remained residential, at least for a much greater length of time.

House building in Bruton Street began in about 1738 as an initiative by the 1st Lady Berkeley and her son William, the 4th Baron, providing dwellings for the gentry of the period. A number of houses on both the north and the south side have been attributed to architect Isaac Ware. After travels in Italy he was employed in 1729 as clerk of works at Windsor Castle. Later on, he published *The Complete Body of Architecture* in 1756 and was an authority on the work of Andreo Palladio, the influential Italian architect. (The Palladian style, named after him, adhered to classical Roman principles.)

Not all was sweetness and light in Bruton Street. In 1760 a crone of a milliner, Mrs Sarah Meteyard with her daughter, also Sarah, employed a sickly child, Anne Naylor. Unable to do her work and after attempts to flee her employers, Anne suffered almost every physical indignity. She was beaten, locked up, starved, tied and unable to sit or kneel, and afterwards she died. Her body was hidden in the garret until the smell became overpowering and then it was disposed of in Chick Lane. Eventually mother and daughter were convicted of murder and both took the road to The Tyburn Tree, where they were executed.

Today the north side of Bruton Street is adorned in an exclusivity derived from a mix of two very specialised businesses. Art and fashion, or rather haute couture, sit very happily side by side, almost alternating in their presence as one goes from Berkeley Square to Bond Street. Art galleries have enjoyed being located in this area for many years and it was thought at one time that the fashion industry might displace it. Art, however, remains big business. The eclectic nature of the product and its potential to combine pleasure with investment, for those who can afford it, is reason enough for this industry to thrive.

Osborne Samuel, of 23A Bruton Street is a partnership of two galleries formed in 1994, specialising in 20th-century art. Their collections resemble a roll-call of many of the most distinguished sculptors and artists of the period. E & R Cyzer, which also specialises in 20th Century art, is at No 23.

Halcyon Gallery has two premises in Bruton Street, Nos 24 and 29, and a further one at 29 New Bond Street. They state a commitment to supporting and nurturing outstanding living artists. At the time of writing the Bruton Street galleries presented very different displays. The burnished bronzes at No 29 contrasted starkly with a rough-hewn, white plaster, female torso impaled upon a St Andrew's Cross, displayed in the window at No 24.

Norman Hartnell, the famous couturier, established his business in Bruton Street in 1923. He was very much a favourite of the Royal family and has the distinction of being the first British dress designer to take a show to Paris. His name remains emblazoned on the wall of No 26 even though his label and brand have moved to Savile Row.

Diane von Furstenberg at No 25 displays her fashions on beautiful mannequins dressed in a palette of bright colours, as though at a picnic in the country. The only missing element is perhaps the polo match they might have been attending. Further down the road at No 28, Mathew Williamson's original collection can be seen stretching to the rear of the shop. The boast 'Fake Landscapes' inscribed on his window beneath his name defies understanding.

Should art and fashion not be sufficiently fulfilling for a lifestyle of some elegance, then Ronald Phillips Ltd at No 26 and Antoine Cheneviere at No 27 are at hand with antiques and antique furnishings of great style and quality.

At No 30 Bruton Street, and a relatively new kid on the block in the world of designer clothing, is 'Stella McCartney', with each letter of the name picked out with pink party lights. Stella McCartney, daughter of Beatle, Sir Paul McCartney, has a Parisian resonance with Norman Hartnell in that she was trained in Paris. Whilst her clothes no doubt fascinate the aficionados, it is the strong smell of sandalwood and the macro marquetry of the wall coverings that have an immediate appeal.

Slightly out of context, though thoroughly well established is the presence of the gunsmiths Holland & Holland at Nos 31 and 33 Bruton Street, founded by Harris Holland in 1835. Reports indicate that Harris Holland started out in the wholesale tobacco business spending his leisure time shooting pigeon and grouse. One can only presume that he and his friends were somewhat dissatisfied with the weapons available at the time and he set about making them himself. He was good at what he did and what appeared to have started as a sideline gradually became a real business. Early guns bore the inscription H Holland and were probably built to his design. It was later that he took on his nephew Henry as an apprentice who eventually became a full partner in 1887 when it became Holland & Holland.

*Top and bottom right: The guns of gunsmith
Holland & Holland.*

Sandwiched between The Holland & Holland houses is the discreet Georgian frontage of Brioni, Umberto Angeloni's luxury Italian men's outfitters. This is Berkeley Square's challenge to Savile Row. Indeed the company was founded in 1945 on the basis of combining the quality of Savile Row tailoring with the flair of the emerging Italian fashion industry.

Ms McCartney is representative of yet one more coincidence allowing Bruton Street to bask in the reflected glory of the two most famous pop groups of all time. Just down the road at No 34a, Rolling Stone Ronnie Wood has a delightful art gallery called Scream, with its fast-moving exhibitions, that appears to concentrate on modern, potentially offbeat artists.

This page and opposite page:
Shop fronts in Bruton Street.

As mentioned on page 95, No 17, sadly demolished to make way for Berkeley Square House and presumably Jack Barclay, belonged at one time to the Earl of Strathmore, father of Elizabeth Bowes-Lyon. As Duchess of York, it was here that Elizabeth lived and on 26 April 1926, she gave birth to Princess Elizabeth, now Queen Elizabeth II. Like many houses of this period, it is not easy to determine who was responsible for its design. However, the name Shepherd crops up with great regularity in the building history of the West End of London. It is John Shepherd who appears to have much to do with the building of No 17. This man had a reputation for being drunk from morning to night and cared little for his workmen. It was fortunate for John that his brother Edward, of Shepherd Market fame, was much more talented and reliable. Edward took over John's responsibilities and saved him from insolvency. Having inherited a shell of a building he exercised his skills and knowledge of the arts of plasterwork to create one of the grander Palladian houses in London.

It would appear that Lord Cadogan first took up residence in 1742 in time for the new London season and perchance saving John Shepherd from bankruptcy. The 4th Earl of Plymouth lived there from 1762 until 1797 when the Earl of Rosebery took over for about four years. Then for 20 years, at the start of the 19th century, Henry Luttrell the 2nd Earl of Carhampton spent his final years, having formerly been a soldier and politician. To add just a little comedy to the succession, a distant relative of the Duke of Wellington, rejoicing under the name of The Hon William Pole-Tynley-Long-Wellesley and son of the Earl of Mornington, dwelt there but failed to pay the rates and absconded into obscurity.

Opposite page: Bruton Street where it joins Berkeley Square.

The house remained empty for about eight years or so before Sophia, Lady Rendlesham, a widow, stayed until her death in 1853. Lord Beaumont lasted but one year and, in 1854, the house became that of Viscount Ebrington son of Earl Fortescue. There followed a succession of short-term occupants all with rather grand names, except for one, a John Parry Jones, who sold No 17 to Claude George Bowes-Lyon, maternal grandfather of Queen Elizabeth II whose family were the last to live there. In 1929, the Canadian Pacific Railway used it for office accommodation and later the demolition men came in to make way for Berkeley Square House.

1 BRUTON STREET

No 1 Bruton Street is an address to remember. Sited on the corner it is possibly one of London's most modern listed buildings. A recent article in *The New York Times* referred to the building as boring. It is far from that. The square concrete structure of the 1950s could so well have been just that, with the exception that the original developers Time Life commissioned at least five of the greatest contemporary artists of the time to decorate this architectural statement: Henry Moore, Ben Nicholson, Salvador Dali and Geoffrey Clarke RA to name but four. In itself, it represents a cautionary tale.

The Time Life Building was listed by Westminster City Council in 1988. By 1993, when Time Life were to leave the building, the council decreed that the works of art (purchased by Time Life), were components of the building and were not to be removed. It is possible that this debate is still ongoing. Whilst there is no argument about the Moore stonework screen, and possibly the Dali sculpture surmounting the door, there must surely be some question over the others. Decorating the stairwell is a huge Ben Nicholson painting. In the foyer is a tear-drop tree sculpture, unattributed, and before the staircase is Geoffrey Clarke's iron arrangement believed to be called 'Complexions of Man'.

It is in the roof garden that a spectacular reclining figure in all its Moore-ish glory gives grace and elegance to this space. It represents an unlikely juxtaposition of a timeless great work of art decorating an improbable picnic area for the 500 or so who work at the desks of Hermes and other companies within the building.

Opposite page, top: Henry Moore's 'Reclining Figure' on the roof garden of the Time Life building.

Opposite page, bottom: The Salvador Dali sculpture above the doorway.

Above: The Henry Moore roof garden screen.

BRUTON PLACE

The houses on the east side of Berkeley Square were slightly less grand than those to the west. One can imagine the 18th-century's estate agents proclaiming those on the west being substantial town dwellings for the aristocracy, complete with on-site accommodation for staff and stabling for several carriages and their horses. For those properties on the east side, however, the copy would indicate that such facilities are to be provided off-site. Not a massive inconvenience, simply a slight but significant one. Thus, Bruton Place was the mews accommodation with stables and coach houses for the houses built on the east side of the Square. Even now the sack hoists can be seen on Nos 36 and 38.

Bruton Place is a hockey stick of a mews, the main handle of which runs parallel to Bruton Street. It is a combination of residential property, pubs, restaurants, offices, retail and service outlets. Timothy Taylor, after marrying Lady Helen Windsor, set up his art gallery with its delightful numbered signboard, before moving to Dering Street further away. High-class restaurants help to set the tone of this narrow street. Many reviewers talk with surprise and comment upon the inaccessibility of this cobbled backstreet. Arguably this is part of the charm.

Umu, a Japanese restaurant, is able to claim style, discretion, exclusivity and rare opportunity as it serves an exceptionally high-quality traditional Japanese menu and can boast being as attractive to businesswomen as businessmen. A bigger boast must surely be that it has over 130 sake drinks listed on its menu, ranging from fresh, through rich, to dessert and sparkling sake.

Top: Sack hoist.

Bottom: Numbered sign.

Right: Bruton Place.
Watercolour by David Thompson 2008.

Alongside is Bellamy's, boasting a high-class French cuisine, an oyster bar and a takeaway delicatessen. Once again the highest quality would appear to be on offer and the word gracious has been used when describing the leather, the starched linen and the service. Further towards Berkeley Square and next to the Guinea Grill is Greig's, another restaurant of fine reputation, not least for its food and the stateliness of the three oak-panelled dining rooms. Greig's appears to concentrate upon the best of British fare and makes claim to serving the best steaks in town. Not least they are known for providing good value for money. There is a rumour that the rivalry between the Guinea Grill and Greig's was at one time so intense that doormen would fight to open cab doors to usher folk into their preferred eating house.

Opposite page and above: Unspoilt architectural features in Bruton Place.

Left: Horses' heads in brick-work relief above Bellamy's Restaurant.

Lilliman & Cox, at No 34, must surely be one of the most exclusive dry cleaners in the whole of the United Kingdom. Tucked away in this mews terrace it breathes a competence and excellence in one of the more unspectacular components of the service industry. In 1946 a master tailor, Sidney Lilliman from Nottingham, with colleague Arthur Cox recognised a gap in the market. They sited their business in the centre of London's couture circuit and specialised in cleaning the elaborately boned and beaded evening gowns of the day. Their skills were recognised by the royal family, being awarded warrants from not only Her Majesty the Queen but also the late Queen Mother and HRH the Prince of Wales. The company's reputation spread worldwide with many customers from the world of entertainment. Famously Marilyn Monroe sent her screen costumes here for cleaning.

In total resonance with the rather exclusive nature of Berkeley Square is a gentlemen's hairdresser, Gentlemen's Tonic at 31 Bruton Place. Their aim is to combine the traditional barbershop with elements of the modern. Among the leather, mahogany and marble of the old, LCD screens and high-tech music facilities are available at what are described as private haircutting stations. Gentlemen's Tonic boasts a philosophy they describe as understated, but ensuring the highest level of care and attention.

A complete square tunnel of white walls, white light and white models stands out in stark contrast to the Georgian mews frontage of this street where Horden Cherry Lee, architects, at 34 Bruton Place demonstrate their wide range of spectacular modern designs.

The common theme would appear to be white and glass vertical surfaces. Their 'microcompacthome', a one-room, one-loo cubic living unit, was at one time temporarily erected in Berkeley Square. It was an expression of architecture, sculpture and utility all in one. Curiously they share the same street number as Lilliman & Cox and the rather quaint arrangement seems to work.

Within the concentration of art galleries in this small corner of London, Sladmore at No 32, has its contemporary gallery here in Bruton Place. It is, by reputation, a leading sculpture gallery with over 40 years' experience dealing with fine bronzes from 1850 to the present day.

On the opposite side of the mews is David Aaron's ancient arts and rare carpet gallery, sitting impressively on the corner of Bruton Place at No 22 Berkeley Square. Though its spacious showrooms display the works of cultures displaced by both time and distance from the hubbub outside, it is situated exclusively and comfortably close to other galleries.

COMMERCE AND WEALTH

Those great Georgians, as founding fathers of the most enviable lifestyle created by mankind, might just look upon their successors in Berkeley Square with many feelings ranging from scorn to anger. Where did it all go wrong they might just be asking one another. They might forgive, or even applaud, the 21st-century desire to make more than an honest crust, but to do so in surroundings designed to respond to the comfort and pampering of almost every human need might be seen as being unforgivable. These were the homes of the great and the good and each one was a focus of social engineering. One aspect was that of employing relatively large numbers of men and women in domestic service. The principal role, however, was to create a climate and in the current vernacular, a network for their residents to rule the world. It did this reasonably well and in relative comfort. Perhaps little has really changed, though there are great changes of emphasis. The ruling classes no longer have titles shored by patronage. The currency is financial power in the global market place. Many of the great houses look the same as they did 200 to 300 years ago but now they are almost without exception offices or shops. Mainly they are offices.

Perhaps there were two significant events. The first was the pulling down of Devonshire House, making provision for commercial properties in 1924. The second in 1936 was the razing to the ground of most of the eastern side of the Square to make way for Berkeley Square House allowing the rise of the largest office accommodation in Europe at that time.

Today there is just one property in the whole of Berkeley Square dedicated to residential use; the remainder are commercial enterprises.

It is not easy to plot the descent into commerce of the whole area but there is little doubt that, from the mid Eighties until now, almost a decade after the millennium, commerce has grown and grown. This is simply what happened. Upmarket estate agents, high-street banks, even quality car salesmen and high-class service industries had already pitched their tents and they were followed by a number of high-worth companies such as British Airways, SmithKline Beecham and BP, all with town-house headquarters. It is possible that as shareholders gathered more power and influence in the corporate governance of their companies they considered such facilities as an unnecessary expenditure. It seemed to become a fashion, as these blue-chip companies started moving out in the Nineties.

Some, like BP, with offices in Hill Street, owned a relatively large portfolio of commercial property. In the mid Nineties, informal reports suggest there were around 45 empty town houses in the area. Towards the end of the decade, the financial climate changed considerably with the advent of the hedge fund and before that the PC, the personal computer. An intelligent businessman needs only a telephone, a desk, a roof over his head and a computer to start up in business. With these four components he or she is set fair for making money and in particular within the industry of finance and banking. Mayfair started to take off with the installation of many small but high-worth businesses. In this world of international finance a great many American companies settled. There are presently some 36 American private equity companies within the Berkeley Square Estate.

What is it that attracts such businesses to the West End in preference to the City? A simple answer could be that, because business is global, it is useful to have hotels at hand and Mayfair boasts the very best. Also, with the exception of Livery Company activity, the City of London dies at night in contrast to Mayfair's great kaleidoscope of activity for every taste at whatever time.

There would seem to be very little chance, for the grand houses in and around Berkeley Square, of their ever reverting to greater residential use. Economic factors are so strongly biased towards commercial use, what with business rates being several orders of magnitude greater than residential rates. There is clear evidence of the highest standards of maintenance and refurbishment, as offices are converted to the open-plan spaces used universally today in the working environment.

One question beggars an obvious answer. If one man with one computer and his desk, is able to work effectively anywhere in the world, why does he descend, with a myriad of cohorts, upon one small area of town, like seagulls upon a cliff face?

THE WESTERN ESTATE

'Lord Chatham with his sword undrawn
Kept waiting for Sir Richard Strachan.
Sir Richard longing to be at 'em
Kept waiting too, for whom? Lord Chatham.'
'Morning Post', February 1810 (Lord Chatham lived at 10 Charles Street).

The western Estate includes Charles Street, Hill Street and Farm Street. Building began in Charles Street in the mid-1700s. Whilst Messrs Cock and Hillyard concentrated most of their effort on buildings within the Square and to the east, it was the master carpenter John Phillips who built much of the housing within Charles Street. He established his own workshop at number 27A Charles Street and, with bricks being made but a stone's throw away in the Berkeley's Bricklands, he was well placed to develop the area. A number of his houses remain on both sides of the road.

Hill Street takes its name from the original Hay Hill Farm. It all began as dwelling places of the highest quality for those able to afford and aspire to the most genteel of lifestyles imaginable. Today almost every building, without exception, is dedicated to business and commercialisation. A few properties have been converted into flats. At first glance it appears to be a street of fine houses and, upon further inspection, it is clear that almost every house has a balcony. There are balconies in abundance of all shapes and sizes, zigging and zagging higher or lower in the buildings, installed on what seems to be an architectural whim. Victorians, let alone Georgian folk, were not in the habit of taking tea 'al fresco' in town. Firstly, the weather was always a hazard and, secondly the Victorian industrial haze was a positive danger to health. The balcony feature must surely have been included as a simple adornment and possibly something exotic and continental. Hill Street was being built at about the same time as Charles Street and both streets benefited by having the 'service' street, Hays Mews, between them, to provide for stabling and coach housing.

There is little to be said historically for Farm Street, except that it really was a street leading to or from the Hay Hill Farm. In the present day this elegant street could not be further distanced from its bucolic heritage. Much of it remains residential with Farm House in particular rivalling both the Church of the Immaculate Conception and the Punch Bowl public house for attention. This very attractive private dwelling with its mock Tudor beams exists, seemingly, simply to give surprise. Further along to the west is the only school in the whole of the Berkeley Square Estate. It is that of Saint George's and named after the parish church in Hanover Square. With a history going back to the beginning of the 19th century, the present school buildings go back to 1897, though it was not until 1931 that the boys and girls departments were amalgamated into a mixed school. Segregation of the sexes was an important component of early schooling during the evolution of state education and the separate boys' and girls' entrances to the school remain in evidence today.

*Right: Farm Street
from the top of
Berger House.*

45 Charles Street

Lady Dorothy Nevill, society hostess and horticulturist lived at No 45. She was almost the Dorothy Parker of her time, bequeathing memorable quotations to posterity. Famously she said: 'The real art of conversation is not only to say the right thing at the right place but to leave unsaid the wrong thing at the tempting moment.' Perhaps her greatest social achievement was to entertain both Gladstone and Disraeli at her table for lunch on the same occasion.

42 Charles Street

George Bryan Brummell was born 7 June 1778 in London and was better known as Beau Brummell. He was an arbiter of fashion in Regency England and a friend of the Prince Regent. He led the trend for men to wear understated, well-cut clothes. He introduced the cravat as neckwear for men and in passing brought to fashion the modern man's suit now worn with a necktie. His style of dress came to be known as dandyism. Falling out with the Prince of Wales was Brummell's downfall. He once remarked to a friend: 'Alvanley, who's your fat friend?' (Referring to Prince George, who had snubbed him a moment earlier.)This probably did not help. Brummell lived in France for the rest of his life dying penniless and insane from syphilis in Caen in 1840.

40 Charles Street

Lady Monkton famously lived here in 1786 and married the Earl of Cork and Orrery in her own sitting room by special licence.

This page and opposite top and bottom: The doorways in Charles Street opened up to the richest of social lives in Georgian and Victorian times.

One of the more notable grand houses is Dartmouth House at No 37, which is an amalgam of three houses. This was achieved in 1890 for Lord Revelstoke, the only Baring to receive a peerage principally because he was a banker. The others had been politicians or public servants. Edmund, known as Ned, became Lord Revelstoke in 1885, when London was the undisputed financial capital of the world. Revelstoke father and son ran Barings for 50 years, and they were considered a formidable pair. Both were reported as being: 'intelligent and cultivated, self-confident to the point of arrogance. They were dignified in manner and imposing in appearance, men accustomed to demanding the deference of their inferiors, putting into that category the generality of mankind.' But Ned Baring also had a streak of recklessness inherited from his grandfather, and a gambler's instinct (his father won his Mayfair house at a game of cards). He was a generous man, and he could afford to be: his annual income was £100,000, worth £6,100,000 today.

Dartmouth House is now home of the English Speaking Union (ESU). Purchased by the ESU in 1926, it is one of the most notable properties in Mayfair and was listed by the Department of Culture, Media and Sport to Grade II, being scheduled as a building of national importance. The building is noted for its magnificent interior that includes grand marble fireplaces, Louis Quatorze walnut panelling, a fine French marble grand staircase, with a superb painted ceiling by Pierre Victor Galland.

Right: The magnificent frontage of Dartmouth House, The English Speaking Union.

Overleaf: Page 165, architecture of Waverton Street.

33 Charles Street

Sydney Smith, former minister of the Berkeley Chapel, lived here. He bought a 14-year lease on the property and called it 'The Hole'!

28 Charles Street

Edward Gibbon was an English historian and Member of Parliament. His most important work, *The History of the Decline and Fall of the Roman Empire*, was published in six volumes. *The History* is one of the most enduring learned works of western civilisation. Gibbon is believed to have suffered from hydrocele testis, a grave condition that causes the testicles to engorge with fluid. It was an embarrassing condition and difficult to hide, leading Gibbon to withdraw from society. After a series of unsuccessful treatments he finally succumbed at the age of 56. A fitting epitaph described him as the 'English giant of the Enlightenment'.

24 Charles Street

John Hoppner was an English painter of German descent, born in London who lived at No 24 at the turn of the 19th century. He was the son of a German lady-in-waiting to Queen Charlotte, wife of King George III, which led to some speculation at the time that he may have been his son, though this has never been proved. Early on he trained as a chorister at the Chapel Royal, though later choose to reject singing in favour of enrolling at the Royal Academy to study art. He became an established portrait painter, whose court connections earned him many prestigious sitters. His son, Richard Belgrave Hoppner, also became a painter, but chose to specialise in marine scenes rather than portraiture.

22 Charles Street

The Duke of Clarence, later King William IV, lived at No 22 from 1826 which was later the home of Admiral Sir Edward Codrington, the victor of Navarino. It was the future 'Sailor King' who encouraged the Admiral Codrington in his victory at Navarino: 'Go to it Ned, and smash these damned Turks!'

20 Charles Street

Lord Rosebery was born at No 20 in 1847. Later in life he set up residence at No 38 Berkeley Square from where he exercised his power and influence becoming not only Prime Minister but also chairman of the London County Council, a post held by Ken Livingstone and abolished by Margaret Thatcher making him the last incumbent. It was not to be known at the time that Mr Livingstone was to go on and become the first Mayor of London.

*Opposite page and right: Chesterfield Hill,
named after Lord Chesterfield, the 18th century
politician and man of letters. It is the only
residential road running from north to south.*

*Above: Beware of the French cat at
3 Red Lion Yard!*

12 Hill Street

Before moving to Berkeley Square the renowned Admiral John Byng lived in No 12, which is, sadly, now a plain modern building covering Nos 12 to 18.

22 Hill Street

Living at No 22, Henry Brougham, later Lord Chancellor in Lord Grey's famous Whig government, was responsible for, among other things, the Slavery Abolition Act of 1833.

24 Hill Street

Mrs Elizabeth Montagu was a British social reformer, patron of the arts, hostess, literary critic and writer who helped organise and lead the bluestocking society. Both her parents were from wealthy families with strong ties to the British peerage and intellectual life. She married Edward Montagu, a wealthy man with extensive holdings, to become one of the richest women of her era. She devoted her energies to fostering English and Scottish literature, and to the relief of the poor.

This page, opposite page and pages 164 and 165: Beautiful railings and the Italianate balconies of Hill Street, forever unused in London's hostile climate.

PUBLIC HOUSES AND DRINKING PLACES

'... ran about the room and roared;
I might have simply sat and snored-
I rose politely in the Club
And said, "I feel a little bored;
Will someone take me to a pub?"
'A Ballade of an Anti-Puritan', G K Chesterton.

The Berkeley Square Estate is well served with a generous number of public houses and many of them blessed with a history going back three centuries or more. Without exception all of the pubs mentioned go back on a time scale that is measured in centuries and is something that only confirms an undisputed claim on the importance of the dispensing of ale and spirits upon the welfare, development and history of not just this area, but the whole of the United Kingdom.

Towards the middle of Bruton Street is the very famous Guinea public house, boasting a provenance going back to the 15th century. Its design has much in common with the House of Commons which is said to have fewer seats than members in order to create an atmosphere of crowding and expectation on important occasions. So the Guinea, with its central bar, which seems to take up a great deal of room, creates cheerfulness and warmth as customers crowd in to attract the attention of the barmaid.

This page and page 169: The Guinea in Bruton Place, established in 1423.

Opposite page: The Red Lion in Waverton Street.

Page 168: The Punch Bowl in Farm Street.

The Red Lion, built in 1752, is towards the western edge of the Estate, in a quiet corner overlooked by the green timber shiplap of Carpenter House and there on the wall at the bottom of Waverton Street, a pointing finger is inscribed to assist the City of Westminster street sign announcing the way to Charles Street. Should one resist the temptation to venture through its extremely narrow access, the Red Lion, tucked in the corner of Waverton Street with Charles Street, is immediately available at one's right hand to offer refreshment.

By reputation, it was a country pub and, being close to the Hay Hill Farm of old, there is every reason for this being so. As times changed with the urbanisation of Mayfair it became the hostel of those in service in the fine homes of its inhabitants, and was also used extensively by the builders of Berkeley Square, Hill Street and Charles Street. Butlers and boot boys downing their regular pints of porter might hope to cast an eye upon an 'in-between maid', sneaking a rare moment of freedom away from the demands of her mistress. On into the 20th century the Red Lion became the haunt of business folk. The sidewalk near the pub is so narrow one must step out into the street to get around waste bags left overnight for collection. Reaching for the door brings a sense of stepping back in time. Tucked away in a quiet corner of Mayfair it enjoys a relatively tranquil life still with the looks and feel of a country pub. A century later it is completely surrounded by what has become the most expensive real estate in London. Nonetheless, it retains a rustic charm with its low ceiling, dark panelled walls, wooden floors and antique windows. Winged settles and stools make up the majority of the furniture in the single bar, and there is a charming restaurant area to the rear. Though off the beaten track, the Red Lion is invariably busy at lunchtimes and early evenings. It has been reported that singer Tom Jones said this was his favourite London pub.

The Coach & Horses in Hill Street was established in 1744 and is Grade II listed. The front facia was rebuilt in 1850. Formerly it was an inn surrounded by coach houses and stables which are now mews houses. Until the time of cars, the Coach & Horses used to supply comfortable lodgings for aristocracy on their journey through London. After World War I, it stopped providing lodgings and became the pub one can see today. Many original features still remain, including cellars, larders and coal rooms under Hill Street and Hays Mews. Many of the licensees were female. One, Elizabeth Coddington, was landlady from 1881 to 1898. Her husband was a coachman and ran his business from the Coach & Horses while she ran the inn.

*Opposite page and this page: The Coach
& Horses in Hill Street at the corner of
Hay's Mews.*

*Above: Early print of The Only Running
Footman sign. in Charles Street.*

*Right: The Only Running Footman in
Charles Street.*

Opposite page: The Punch Bowl in Farm Street.

'The Only Running Footman' is colloquially known as 'The Running Footman', and is one of the historic public houses in the area. It takes its name from the very last of the running footmen who was reported to have been retained in employment long after footmen's true usefulness had been overtaken by the introduction of street lighting. It has had a recent facelift but maintains its old world charm. The long wooden bar and comfortable seating booths complemented by good food do much to enhance its reputation.

Tucked away in Farm Street is the charming little tavern, the Punch Bowl. It is yet another building looking more suited to the country than Central London. Built in the 1750s it would have been a country pub, as undoubtedly it was built to provide comfort and solace to the farmhands who worked Hay Hill and other farms in the community. It boasts being the second oldest pub in Mayfair. Window boxes and hanging baskets decorate the wooden frontage. Double doors open into the single bar, which is plain and simple, with bare floorboards and darkened timber panelling. As with all these old pubs one should take note of the old, and possibly valuable, prints that line walls and staircases, providing insights into the individual history of the inns themselves.

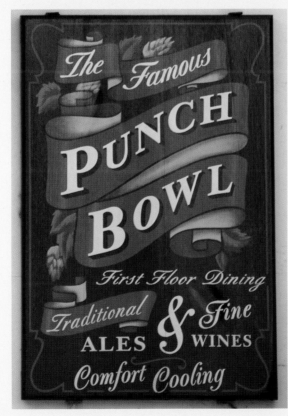

The second Coach & Horses public house on this patch of Mayfair is in Bruton Street, just off Bond Street. It is a tall and quaintly shaped building described by one reviewer as 'Tudorbethan'. Its triangular shape is constrained by the subterranean flow of the River Tyburn. It provides real ales and has a reputation of being unpretentious and good value. The menu even boasts a dish, 'Posh Bacon & Eggs'.

Opposite page and below: The Coach & Horses in Bruton Street.

A DAY IN THE LIFE

'My rule always was to do the business of
the day, in the day.'
Arthur Wellesley - Duke of Wellington.

Stride out onto the pavements of Berkeley Square on any day and little appears to happen, or can be seen to happen, to identify the role of this elegant part of west London in modern life. From Piccadilly in the south, to Mount Street at the northern end, it boasts four high-quality car sales rooms yet only rarely does one see customers emerging proudly to drive off in motor carriages that suspend concern for the size of their carbon footprint. That is not quite true as, on one occasion, a family emerged with camelhair-coated Mama and bejewelled baseball-capped teenagers, materialised through the plate-glass doors of Jack Barclay's showrooms and dissapeared into the open doors of an expensively number plated Rolls Royce. The thrill was to see the excitement on the faces of the children.

In the City, jobbers, brokers and bankers cry aloud their business as they scurry to and fro and seem to be possessed of a financial body language; in Berkeley Square this does not happen, even though some say its corporate wealth and investment matches that of the City. Common activity is confined to the summer months when the benches, so generously donated by scores of American benefactors, seat the young who take their lunch economically with a sandwich and bottled water. Others lie on the green grass and soak up the sun. These represent but a fraction of those that work here. Office accommodation is varied in its frontage from the austere penitential brickwork of Berkeley Square House via the London 'flat or office' architecture that sits above the Bank of Ireland or to the buildings of Mr Berger and the like who built their offices in the Forties and Fifties in the northeast corner of the square. The fortunate are those who work in the buildings that retain much of their Georgian and Victorian glory. Look closer within and, with the exception of chairmen and chief executives, most workers share open-plan accommodation. Sit on one of the benches and you can witness the whole range of support activity in action, almost totally uncoordinated but geared to maintain order.

Opposite page, this page and pages 182 to 187: Observations of a day in the life of Berkeley Square. 'Joggers jog, postmen deliver, chauffeurs wait, dispatch riders dismount ...'

Westminster Council gardeners gently tend to grass and gravel with orders, no doubt, to be neat but not gaudy. Others from the private sector risk their necks and other parts of their anatomy as, from their white vans, they leap railings to transplant, water and weed window boxes, hanging baskets and railing displays of lobelia and other busy floral displays. Joggers jog, postmen deliver, chauffeurs wait, dispatch riders dismount and the ex-communicated smokers find a corner from which to indulge their habit. The pubs fill at lunchtime both inside and out and all seems well with the world. At night, bouncers bounce, but so gently. Only Annabel's sees fit to employ such security. Their green over-coated sentinels busy themselves as car door openers. Could it be they are descended from the last of the running footmen? Though this species passed into obscurity as a result of the introduction of the motor vehicle, the 'health and safety at work' inspectors would have had a field day with them, as they insisted upon it being safe to dowse their lanterns of burning tar and tallow in the link extinguishers still in place above the doorkeepers' heads.

Above: 'Roosevelt and Churchill' by Lawrence Holofcener (1995) sit with A N Other.

Opposite page: A street artist finds a quiet doorway.

Each part of Mayfair has a character of its own. From south of Oxford Street and below, through Bond Street to Piccadilly, it is bustling and commercial, concentrating upon the luxury consumer, be it for fashion, art, jewellery, cosmetics, fine arts or antiques. Eastward to Regent Street, the commerce grows, as exclusivity diminishes and tailoring begins to feature more strongly.

Grosvenor Square, dominated by the American Embassy appears to encourage other nations to nestle alongside, creating an atmophere for international diplomacy to thrive. Grosvenor Square itself proclaims that 'special relationship' with our allies across the Atlantic. Park Lane needs to do little to reinforce its reputation for elegance, style and desirability, derived from the game of Monopoly.

And we are left with Berkeley Square. Most significantly it is an extremely mobile part of London. Whilst financiers beaver away behind closed doors, whilst antiquarians contemplate and purchase great works of art, whilst the cloth is cut to the tentative pencil sketches of the dress designer and whilst all this work goes on behind closed doors, equally busy and for all to see are the developers with their builders. Perhaps it is these same builders who are the true descendants of those who made Berkeley Square what it is today. It is an organic community of building and buildings, constantly changing to service incremental changes in purpose. Lord and Lady Berkeley of Stratton were probably the first property developers in this part of London W1, who started by employing Messrs Cock and Hillyard to build their estate. Perhaps those we see every day, in yellow coats behind shuttering or on scaffolding, are their sons.

This page and opposite: Passion, promotion and fun in Berkeley Square.

190

This page and opposite: Visitors passing through Berkeley Square.

Overleaf: Life, luxury, tradition and rest.

'I went away towards Hyde Park ... in the tour, I passed an amazing scene of new foundations,
not of houses only, but as I might say of new cities, new towns, new squares, and fine buildings,
the like of which no city, no town, nay no place in the world can show; nor is it possible to
judge where or when they will make an end or stop of building ...'
An eyewitness in a newspaper report of 1725. ('Berkeley Square to Bond Street', B H Johnson.)

When Horace, the builder's odd-job man, was helping to erect one of several sheds in our garden in Devon, during moments of decision making or compromise he would conclude: 'Best side towards London'. I can imagine Mr Cock and Mr Hillyard arriving at similar conclusions as their urbanisation of the great metropolis began gently spreading westward during the latter half of the 18th century. Significant too was the delegation awarded to such humble folk in an era when architecture was in its heyday and giving rise to the great gestures and creations earlier on, of Sir Christopher Wren, Evelyn and Palladio and later Kent, Adam and Chambers, among many. Messrs Cock and Hillyard, with the Shepherd brothers and perhaps the Cubitts, plus a few others were the journeymen builders who may well have built their houses with hardly a drawing seeing the light of day. What they had was a tradition of elegance, style and quality upon which their craft of house building, for it was a craft, was founded. Architecture was an art form established to respond to the praise of God, the state, or the aristocracy; St Paul's Cathedral, Greenwich and Chelsea Hospitals and the early terrace of palaces lining Piccadilly are witness to this. Building houses was the work of artisans.

That which is Berkeley Square today still has its best side towards London. The west side of the square cries aloud the elegance in size and proportion of what was originally domestic housing and it faces the City of London. It remains forever a testament to those who settled in and developed Mayfair during and after the restoration of the Monarchy.

It is too easy to say simply that all was downhill after the first period of building, but changes in lifestyle over the centuries gave rise to other change in many and various ways. Having said that, these changes were gradual, almost exponential. The fact that an Admiral's pay remained the same from 1790 to 1850 and beyond, suggests that inflation was a word that failed to have any influence on the life of the Georgians and early Victorians. What seemed to flourish was wealth and, with it, influence. The engine of this success was the Empire. Built upon this success was an expanding governing class, whether it governed politically or industrially, it matters not, it governed. It influenced the lives of others, it ruled. To rule it needed access to the seat of power, which in turn meant optimising on the principle means of communication, which was that of speech. In simple terms, those who exercised power needed to talk and in order to talk they needed to live relatively close to one another. This was the determining factor, which, until the turn of the 20th century in 1900, meant the majority of great families in the United Kingdom had great houses in the country and homes in Mayfair.

It is during the 20th century, with its world-changing advances in almost every field of activity: industrial, transport, and not least its use of electrical power, that marks the significant changes to the landscape of Berkeley Square and its surrounds. In this era the change from domestic use of property to business use has taken place. Just 20 years into the last century, the Duke of Devonshire realised that his Georgian pile, which replaced that of Lord Berkeley, was of more use to his family and heirs as real estate rather than housing. He was not wrong, the industrial revolution had gathered great pace, mechanised warfare had brought havoc to at least two generations. What use would Green Park Underground Station be to the Duke and Duchess of Devonshire? The new Devonshire House development was to provide, in its own right, a whole township's worth of commercial, social and domestic activity. These large family palaces were by then, unfortunately, dinosaurs waiting for extinction.

There is of course a sadness to relate, being the regret that there were no Messrs Cock and Hillyard around to ensure even a measure of style and quality in the performance of the modernisation. A cynic might conclude, that whilst other parts of London needed the bombing of the Blitz to provide the spur for post World War II regeneration, the planners and builders of the 1930s were happy just to 'bomb' their own backyards.

What is unforgivable is that the architects and developers of the Thirties were prepared to delude themselves and others by exaggerating proportion and finish when presenting the case for change.

In the 50, and more, years since World War II, considerable restraint has been shown. The biggest incentive for change, possibly, has been the widening gap between business and residential local authority rates. No local government officer in his right mind would ever turn down an application for change of use of a property from residential to business use. There are now very few residential properties within the triangle of the Berkeley Square Estate. Equally there are no grand plans, of which one is aware, for massive commercial development. No carbuncles, no Gherkins lurk upon the horizon. Much, if any, development has been internal whereby the myriads of small internal rooms have been transformed to open-plan offices where small armies of employees from traders to typists sit at desks, screen to screen, buttock to buttock.

To cast an eye upon the future is a relatively safe thing to do. Whatever happens, change will be slow. Market forces will dictate modest change. Offices with ceiling height above a certain level attract higher rents, which could give rise to some change. However, the more prevalent philosophy of distant and home working undermines the need for massive increases of office space in metropolitan areas.

The Georgians and Victorians found a need to live close by their peers in order to communicate, to exercise power and to govern. Looking ahead, tomorrow's New Elizabethans and the future Caroleans (under a Charles III), will be able to exercise this power remotely from the comfort of their homes, communicating electronically and with great ease.

Could this be a spur to generate an increase in the number of residential properties in Mayfair? Will the reputation of Carolean domestic architecture be destined to follow that of the Georgians? Is it possible that the tie-less, khaki, black grunge that marks a nadir in contemporary male sartorial elegance might be replaced by a new-world chic to rival the reputation of Beau Brummell and his kin? Is Mayfair ready for such an urban renaissance?

The one true absolute certainty is that the Georgian heritage of the western side of Berkeley Square will be standing proudly in 100 years from now; *deo volente!*

BIBLIOGRAPHY

An Encyclopaedia of London	W Kent, 1951
The History of London Squares	E Beresford Chancellor, 1907
London Street Views 1888-1840, Tallis	Peter Jackson FSA, 1969
London, The Biography	Peter Ackroyd, 2000
The London Blue Plaque Guide 2nd Edition	Nick Rennison, 2003
Berkeley Square to Bond Street	B H Johnson, 1952
The Years of Grandeur	Mary Cathcart Borer, 1975
Blue Plaque Guide to London Homes	Martin Hall, 1976
The Berkeleys of Berkeley Square	Bernard Falk, 1944
Mayfair Madams	Maria Perry, 1999
Mayfair - A Social History	Caroline Kennedy, 1986
Mayfair - A Town within London	Reginald Colby, 1966
Survey of London - Vol 40	F H W Shepherd, 1980
The House in Berkeley Square	Maria Perry, 2003
The Diary of Samuel Pepys	Samuel Pepys, 1660
The London Encyclopaedia	Ben Weinreb and Christopher Hibbert, 1983
Ghosts of London (The West End, South and West)	J A Brooks, 1982
Haunted London	Peter Underwood, 1973
Ghosts of London	Jack Hallam, 1975
Mayfair and Belgravia	G Clinch, 1892